NOAH'S ARK: I Touched It

FERNAND NAVARRA

NOAH'S ARK:
I Touched It

EDITED WITH DAVE BALSIGER

LOGOS INTERNATIONAL / Plainfield, New Jersey

*To those who searched
for Noah's Ark
and to those
who will someday
be successful
in excavating it*

Contents

CONTENTS

Publisher's Foreword

In the remote borderland where Turkey, Iran, and the Soviet Union meet, Mount Ararat's snowcapped peak rises majestically 16,900 feet above sea level, dominating the harsh landscape below. In this region, from the thirteenth to the eighth centuries B.C., flourished the kingdom of Urartu, which has yielded many of its secrets to the archaeologist's spade. Today, nomadic Kurds pasture their sheep on the mountain's ample slopes. The name Ararat, of course, is forever linked with that of Noah, and as such is of more than casual interest to Moslems, Christians, and Jews the world around.

Through the centuries, adventurers and historians have reported that the remains of Noah's Ark are still to be found on the mountain. Among the better-known writers who mentioned the renowned vessel was Flavius Josephus (ca. 37–100 A.D.). Twelve hundred years later, Marco Polo, passing along what the natives told him in his travels, declared that the Ark still rested somewhere on the mountain. During the nineteenth century and the first half of the twentieth, others have reported sighting an ancient wooden ship, partially covered by ice and snow, high on the rugged slope.

Do any of the stories contain truth, or did the sightings result only from inflamed imaginations and wishful thinking? Is there a genuine mystery on Ararat which sober men should investigate? Or does the centuries-old accumulation of tales and legends seem to evaporate into nothing under investigation?

During the past two decades, Fernand Navarra, an industrialist of Bordeaux, France, has stirred renewed interest in the riddle of Ararat. Starting in 1952, he has made repeated ascents and succeeded in finding sizable pieces of hardwood—hewn timbers, not logs or trunks—which he has brought back for inspection by others.

Navarra believes this wood must be part of the ancient vessel. "What else could it be?" he asks. "In all likelihood, these are the remains of the flat hull of the biblical vessel, intact through the years, protected by nature itself. I found this wood on Ararat, the traditional stopping place of the Ark. And this wood, besides being visibly squared, cannot be a plain tree trunk.

"What kind of construction took place on Mt. Ararat at nearly 14,000 feet, almost 5,000 years ago?" he insists. "And if these remains are not those of the Ark, they are still of archaeological interest, since they would be of some unknown construction that no tradition or history mentions anywhere."

Navarra quotes the 5,000-year figure from an analysis of a piece of the wood made by Spain's *Instituto Forestal*, in conjunction with the University of Bordeaux, and reported by them April 7, 1956. According to their study, the age of the wood sample "oscille aux alentours de *cinq mille ans*." However, other age-dating tests have been contradictory. One sample subjected to carbon-14 dating has been assigned an age of only

1,500 years. Obviously, further specimens should be found and tested, and such factors as contamination evaluated.

The publishers of this book make no claims or prophecies as to the outcome of future explorations on Ararat. But they do believe that the story of Navarra's love affair with the famed mountain, his adventures in climbing it, his discovery of wood above timberline on a mountain with few if any trees, is worth the telling. And they trust that if fact, opinion, and legend are kept separate, the narration can prove illuminating and beneficial. Scientists are reserving judgment as to the nature of the discovery. But hewn wood has, in fact, been found high on Ararat as recently as 1969. Let the reader examine the evidence and form his own opinion.

If nothing else, this book is the firsthand report of a courageous man's adventures on a mountain "because it is there." At best, this story could be the prelude to one of mankind's great adventures.

THE PUBLISHERS

Preface

I was five years old when I first heard the story of Noah and the Flood. I had fallen into the water and almost drowned before being fished out. As my mother gave me a rubdown, she related the biblical story of the Deluge and told me that I, like Noah, had been saved from a flood.

As I grew older, my acquaintances said I had a special instinct. They would ask my advice about lost objects and I usually found them. If I had another aptitude, it was a zest for active sports—hiking, climbing, and swimming. Without realizing it, I was getting ready for a life of adventure and discovery.

In 1937 I served in the French military forces in the Middle East. During my days off, I took long walks in the hills above Damascus, accompanied by an Armenian friend, Alim. One day, hiking farther than usual, we started climbing up Mount Hermon. About 1,300 feet from the top, Alim sank to his knees exhausted. I trudged on by myself until I reached the top, an altitude of over 9,000 feet. There I stayed for half an hour viewing the sea of haze and clouds stretching before me under the blue sky and a burning sun. On my way down, I rejoined my companion, and as we walked, he began to tell me his own life story.

"I was born in 1907 on the island in Lake Van," he said. "As a child, I lived there happy with my mother, father, and sister, until 1920. Then my parents moved to Damascus. Before I left Armenia, I went to visit my grandfather in the town of Bayazid, at the foot of Mount Ararat. The old man assured me that Noah's Ark was still on the mountain. 'When I was young,' he told me, 'I once tried to reach it. But I wasn't strong enough in the high altitude and had to give up. I never found it.'

"I promised granddad that I would try, too," continued Alim. "But *you* are the one who should go, Navarra. Mountain climbing does not wear you out the way it does me. I am sure you would bring back a fragment of the Ark."

The idea intrigued me, and I determined to give it a try. But not till fifteen years later did I have my first opportunity to tackle the mountain. Once I was back in France, the war came, then the occupation, and I could not travel. That is, I was prevented from traveling, physically, through space. But no one could keep me from traveling through time with the help of books, to learn all I could about the Deluge and the Ark, to study different traditions and theories, and to compile a list of previous attempts to locate the Ark. This research gave me a background which later proved both fascinating and valuable.

There are many writings about a great Deluge, I discovered.* The Hebrews, of course, have preserved in the Old Testament the story of the worldwide catastrophe. The Greeks told of it in

---

* See Appendix I and II.

fables, to support their mysteries. The Romans had a disguised
form of the story. The Arabs made it ridiculous by old wives'
tales and extravagant explanations. The Jews and Moslems
revered it as a succession of omens and miracles. The Church
Fathers usually found it obscure and treated it as a mystery.

How could one make sense out of such a mess of conflicting
records, tales, and traditions? There was enough confusion to
deter anyone from exploring Ararat with hopes of finding
anything. However, my love of adventure was stronger than my
doubts and fears. When I was able at last to make the trip, I
gladly exchanged a well-stocked library and comfortable chair
for the opportunity to check my assumptions on the mountain
itself.

ACKNOWLEDGMENT

I wish to express my appreciation to Richard H. Utt for his initial efforts in translating my French transcriptions for this book.

F. NAVARRA

NOAH'S ARK: I Touched It

CHAPTER 1

Pioneers on Mount Ararat

*"And the ark rested in the seventh month, on the
seventeenth day of the month, upon the mountains* of
Ararat."* (Gen. 8:4)

The earliest known witness to the continued presence of Noah's
Ark on Mount Ararat was Berose, or Berosus, a Chaldean priest
who wrote histories of Chaldea and Assyria. This ancient stated
that in his time (circa 475 B.C., almost 2,000 years after the
traditional date of the great flood) people still ascended the
mountain and scraped the bituminous coating from the wood of
the Ark. They used the pieces of bitumen as talismans.

Josephus, who lived during the latter part of the first century,
wrote in his *Antiquities of the Jews* that the Armenians call the
place where Noah landed "The Place of Descent; for the ark
being saved in that place, its remains are shown there by the
inhabitants to this day."

---

* The mountains (plural) of Ararat include an area far greater than the
single peak commonly called Ararat today.

Josephus cites other witnesses: "Hieronymus the Egyptian, who wrote the Phoenician Antiquities, and Mnaseas, and a great many more, also make mention of the same. Nay, Nicolaus of Damascus, in his ninety-sixth book, hath a particular relation about them, where he speaks thus: 'There is a great mountain in Armenia, over Minyas, called Baris, upon which it is reported that many who fled at the time of the Deluge were saved; and that one who was carried in an ark came on shore upon the top of it; and that the remains of the timber were a great while preserved.' " St. Theophilus of Antioch confirmed this statement.

In A.D. 330, Jacob, a patriarch of Nisbis, attempted to reach the top. He failed, but according to a legend an angel visited him and gave him a fragment of the Ark. This fragment was reportedly kept in the church of Etchmiadzin, near Ararat, until the building was destroyed by the earthquake of 1829 and the fragment was lost.

William of Ruysbroeck, a Flemish traveler of the thirteenth century, journeyed near the foot of Mount Ararat in 1254 on his way back from an expedition to the Karakoram Range. He wrote that the mountain, which he called "Masis," was "the mother of the world," and that was why nobody could reach the top. *"Super Masis nullus debet ascendere, quia est mater mundi."* This myth of Ararat's inaccessibility circulated for centuries.

Marco Polo (ca. 1254–1324) mentioned the existence of the Ark and described Mount Ararat as a huge mountain, around which one could not travel in less than two days, and whose summit could not be reached because of everlasting snow.

Sir John Maundeville told the story of Jacob of Nisbis, with one variation. The angel did not give the patriarch a fragment of the Ark, but he helped him to climb up the mountain. Jacob himself found and brought back the fragment which was worshiped later in Etchmiadzin. According to Maundeville, many natives boasted that they had seen and touched the Ark, but he remained skeptical. "No one has gone to the top of Mount Ararat since the monk Jacob. It is impossible to believe those who claim they have made the ascent."

Jean Chardin, a seventeenth-century French traveler, mentioned the same miracle story in his *Voyage to Persia and the East Indies*. Chardin seems to have believed the story, marveling that the monk could climb up Mount Ararat, "when in all seasons of the year the mountain is one enormous mass of snow."

In the eighteenth century, Joseph Pitton de Tournefort, a botanist from Aix, France, collected plants on the slopes of Mount Ararat, but he climbed no higher than the second third of the mountain. Some time later, James J. Morier (died 1849), British diplomat and novelist, failed in an attempt to scale the mountain. A pasha from the Turkish town of Bayazid, located at the foot of Ararat, also failed. He had left on horseback with a numerous escort, but had to stop far below the snow zone. When a late eighteenth-century Persian shah offered a large sum of money to the first person who would reach the summit, nobody even attempted the climb.

In 1800 an American, Claudius James Rich, related the unverifiable claims of a certain Aga Hussein, who claimed to have reached the top of the mountain and seen the remains of the Ark.

The history of ascent of Mount Ararat in modern times begins in 1829, with a Russian, Frederic Parrot.

Parrot was a doctor, a professor at Dorpat University, Estonia, and one of the first alpinists. He gave his name to one of the summits of Monte Rosa, in the Pennine Alps. In September,

3

1829, he made his headquarters at the Saint Jacob monastery, situated on the northwestern side of Mount Ararat. Leaving from that point, he made two unsuccessful attempts. Then he transferred his camp to a spot above the Lake of Kip-Gholl, or Lake Kop, near the permanent snowline, and undertook a third expedition, accompanied by two Russian soldiers and three Armenians. Climbing from terrace to terrace, the six men reached the summit, where they found a large, smooth platform they considered wide enough to have been used as a dry dock for the biblical vessel.

The mountain had been conquered, but the legend of inaccessibility remained. Although Parrot was a man of science, and although he published a detailed, believable account of his ascent, nobody in the area believed he had really succeeded. When the monks of Etchmiadzin questioned the Armenians who had accompanied Parrot, they denied their first declarations and said that, although they had climbed very high, they had not reached the summit. They had only glimpsed it, they said. The summit loomed much higher above them.

Five years later another Russian, Spassky Aftomonoff, also climbed Mount Masis, to "ascertain whether it was true that the stars are visible at noon from the top of high mountains."

In July, 1840, following a major earthquake, the Turkish government sent several teams of workers up the mountain in order to build protective barriers against avalanches. One of these teams reported the discovery of the forepart of a very old ship jutting out of a glacier. This part of the ship, they said, was divided into three rooms.

In 1845 the German geologist Hermann Abich, who had already explored the Caucasus Range, undertook the ascent. He

4

failed three times, once when following the same route that Frederic Parrot had used successfully. A fourth attempt, from the southeastern side, proved successful. But in spite of his reputation, Abich could not overcome the local skepticism any better than Parrot had done. He had ascended the eastern summit of Mount Ararat, scarcely lower than the western summit. Because of overcast weather, he did not reach the other peak. Upon his return to Erivan, his native companions, as Parrot's companions had done, swore that from the spot where they had stood, they had seen other higher summits, "which had hidden part of the horizon."

Jules Leclercq, in his *Journey to Mount Ararat*, gives an account of a military expedition undertaken in 1850, with the protection of the Russian government, to complete the triangulation of Transcaucasia. General Khodzko was in command; State Counsellor Khanikhoff, the astronomer Alexandroff, and several Russian officers made up the general staff. They commanded sixty cossacks. The same Armenian who had guided Abich led the column. On July 30, the expedition left the valley of Sardar-Boulakh and made its way slowly, journeying by short stages. Hindered by squalls and storms, they took eighteen days to reach the top of Great Ararat. General Khodzko spent five days at the top, where he completed his triangulation work, sighting the summit of Mount Elbrus 275 miles away toward the northwest, and corresponding by heliographic signals with astronomers installed on Mount Akhdagh, in the middle of the Goktchai Plateau. The astronomer Alexandroff, a victim of the hardships of the ascent, died a few weeks later in Erivan.

"One might think that an expedition with so many people,

leaving no room for the slightest doubt, would have had enough fame to make Mount Ararat's legendary aura vanish completely. Nothing of the kind happened."

The Russian expedition, though official, was so little known that in 1856 the Englishman Seymour, who had attempted the ascent of Mount Ararat from the Turkish side, proclaimed himself its first conqueror.

In 1868, another Englishman, Douglas Freshfield, undertook the ascent. A mountain guide from Chamonix, Francois Devouassoud; a Caucasian interpreter; a man named Tucker; and a caravan of Persians and Kurds accompanied him. Suffering from mountain sickness, Freshfield had to stop at about 10,000 feet. Devouassoud and Tucker climbed alone till they reached 15,750 feet, where they, too, succumbed to fatigue.

In 1876, a third Englishman, James Bryce, a Member of Parliament, succeeded in reaching the top of Mount Ararat alone, without a guide. Suffering like his predecessors from the effects of rarefied air, he kept on climbing and was surprised to find that his sickness decreased as he got higher. He said he felt better at 16,400 feet than at 13,000. At the latter altitude, in the middle of blocks of lava, he saw "a piece of wood about four feet long and five inches thick, which had obviously been hand-hewn."

Needless to say, Bryce, when he talked about his solitary adventure, found no more believers than Abich or Parrot. The venerable Archimandrite of Etchmiadzin shook his head and declared, "It is impossible. Nobody has ever gone there."

In August, 1883, an article in the Chicago *Tribune* announced a much more important discovery than that of Bryce's modest "piece of wood":

A Constantinople newspaper announces the discovery of Noah's Ark. A Turkish expedition searching for the cause of avalanches on Mount Ararat, suddenly found itself in front of a huge carcass in very dark wood emerging from a glacier. When questioned, the neighbouring natives answered that they had known for six years about the existence of this structure, but that they did not dare get too close because they had seen a ferocious-looking ghost peering out the upper window. The Turks, being courageous people, were not stopped by these stories; they decided to push their investigation further. The position of the wreck, deeply embedded in a gorge of Mount Ararat, made the operation terribly dangerous, and it was only at the cost of unbelievable efforts that they succeeded. The Turks recognized the Ark instantly. It was in good condition, only the sides had suffered. One of the members of the expedition who spoke English and had probably read the Bible, saw that the Ark was made of the gopherwood mentioned by the Holy Book, which, as everybody knows, only grows in the Euphrates plains. When they went inside the carcass, painted in brown, the visitors were able to see that the Admiralty's rulings concerning the transportation of horses had been respected: the inside was divided into compartments fifteen feet high. The Turks could go into three of these compartments only, for the others were full of ice. They could not estimate either how far the Ark stretched under the glacier. But if the whole structure happens to be three hundred cubits long, nonbelievers had better behave themselves.

In August, 1890, the Belgian Leclercq, a confirmed alpinist, had to stop 400 yards from the top. The account of his expedition is probably the most detailed we have. He did not claim to have seen the remains of the Ark, but he did not deny its possible existence: "If Mount Ararat still carries remains of the ark," he writes, "it seems that one should expect to find them on the sides of the mountain rather than on the very top, since during the course of centuries, the movement of the glaciers must have carried them down to lower areas."

In 1893, a Nestorian Archbishop (or Archdeacon) by the name of Nourri, exploring the headwaters of the Euphrates River after he had climbed up Mount Ararat, formally declared that he had seen the remains of the Ark. "Only the bow and the stern of the boat were accessible. The central part was caught in the ice. The ark is made of dark-red beams of very thick wood." He measured the boat and found that the dimensions agreed with those given in Genesis. Full of enthusiasm, he formed a company to finance a second expedition with considerable equipment. He intended to bring the Ark down from Mount Ararat, take it to the United States, and exhibit it at the Chicago World's Fair. Nourri finally abandoned the project, either because his shareholders dropped out or because the Turkish government refused to let him "export" the Ark.

After the "Nourri affair," no other known attempt to explore Ararat or find the vessel took place for some time, at least by Western Europeans. But in August, 1916, a Russian aviator, Wladimir Roskovitsky, in charge of a mission north of the Turkish border, reported that as he flew over Mount Ararat he noticed a bluish spot on the eastern side of the snowcovered summit. Flying closer, he found the spot to be a frozen lake. At the end of this lake emerged what the observer thought to be the skeleton of a huge ship. The whole structure he judged to be the size of a city block. A quarter of the wreck was caught in the ice. On the emerged part, one of the sides was ripped open; the other had space for a big double door, one half of which was missing.

Roskovitsky informed his superiors of the discovery, and they proceeded to check it. They flew over the mountain and also viewed the wreck, which they reported to Moscow and Petrograd. Nicholas II gave orders that an expedition be sent.

One hundred and fifty soldiers worked for a month to make the summit relatively accessible. A scientific mission climbed up to the site, measured the dimensions of the Ark, took photographs, cut off samples, and sent everything to Petrograd. All these documents seem to have disappeared during the Russian revolution.

The Roskovitsky affair revived during World War II. Major Jasper Maskelyn, head of the Soviet camouflage services, reported that one of his men flew over Mount Ararat hoping to see what Roskovitsky said he had seen twenty-five years before. The Soviet pilot reported that he spotted the wreck partly submerged in a frozen lake. An expedition sent afterward found the remains of an ancient vessel whose wood resembled charcoal.

Nevertheless, the *Soviet Encyclopedia* defines the story of Noah's Ark as a "legend which is harmful to science."

In 1949, a former missionary from North Carolina, a Dr. John Smith, accompanied by an engineer, a physicist, and a decorator, climbed Ararat. Their expedition, though well-equipped and financed, was a failure.

Dr. Smith's expedition was the last one before those in which I participated. But while we are speaking of the pioneers, we must mention Egerton Sykes. Sykes never climbed Mount Ararat, for the Turkish government refused him permission to enter the military zone. But he has contributed more than anyone else in collecting historical and geographical information on the Ark. A former secretary to the British Embassy in Warsaw, Sykes spent his retirement years compiling and studying documents concerning the Ark and Mount Ararat. He collected 600 items of source material.

CHAPTER 2

First Expedition—1952

i

I had followed the Ark through time, thanks to oral and written traditions, books and men. Now I determined to seek it in space, at the intersection of the surest meridians—that is, on Mount Ararat.

In the spring of 1952 a friend of mine wanted to attempt the ascent of Mount Ararat, but he lacked the money. I offered to furnish the means, and took command of a five-man team. The others who joined us were a retired staff officer who had studied at the Museum of Natural History and at the Musee de l'Homme, and two motion-picture cameramen. One of them was working for a degree in the history of art and ethnography, and the other had just come back from an expedition to Adelie Land, Antarctica, where he had made a color film.

For transportation, we decided to use my car, a Ford, and a trailer I had built for the expedition. The Ford held up to the end; the trailer was not very well made and let us down.

We organized our itinerary together. We would depart from Paris, cross northern Italy, Yugoslavia, Greece, and the Bosporus Strait into Asian Turkey. We would pass through Ankara and continue on to Erzerum and the foot of Mount Ararat—some 5,000 kilometers,* much of it through rough country.

We received little help as we prepared to leave. In fact, almost everyone who knew our plans made fun of us, as did the press. Thanks to the efforts of our retired officer, we received the visas necessary to enter four countries, but we had to leave before we received permission to climb Mount Ararat, located in a military zone. We hoped to get the permits with the help of Ambassador Hermitte, president of the Comite France-Turquie, and of Rechid Saffet Atabinen, president of the Turkish Automobile Club.

At the last minute, we had to install a luggage rack on top of the car to hold two trunks to carry spare cameras and fragile instruments. On Friday, June 13, we left Paris in the Ford, with the trailer jammed full of equipment.

On June 19, at 10:00 A.M., we arrived at the customs station on the edge of the no-man's-land separating the Yugoslav border from Greece.

ii

Scrub land, rocks, dried-up stony creeks, a merciless sun, and a little shade from meager apricot trees—this was our first impression of Greece.

We got through customs without trouble, but the customs

* About 3,000 miles.

officers and two Belgian tourists warned us at length about the condition of the roads. We listened to them, but did not worry. We had had plenty of experience. Only a few miles farther on, we found that they had not exaggerated.

The road dazzled with white gravel, and the pebbles our wheels kicked up sounded like machine-gun bullets under the car. The war had left traces everywhere: ruined houses with burned-out beams, charred railway cars, trenches along the crests of the hills and through the fields. The roads had been mined, and after the mines had been removed, no one had filled the holes, some of which were craters. The bridges shook, or sometimes were lacking altogether. Fortunately, most of the riverbeds had dried up. Often the wheels skidded in the sand, and we had to cut reeds and put them under our wheels for traction.

At last, looking through a mountain pass, we saw the purple sea. Then we followed the paved Marshall highway, which led from Athens to Alexandropolis, along the seashore. We made up for lost time and soon arrived in Salonika.

Next we skirted Lake Bechik, which separated the Chalcidice Peninsula from the mainland. This peninsula extends three mountainous fingers into the Aegean Sea. The eastern finger forms the peak of Mount Athos. Offshore, we saw the Greek islands with their legendary names: Thasos, Imbros, Samothrace—promise of victory. Then Cavala, terraced above the sea, where we found a cove in which to spend the night. Content with our trip thus far, we went to sleep as the sun swung to the west and surrendered its light to the sea.

In the morning, the bad road made us feel humble again. From Dedeagatch, the road was a mere trail. The Ford squeaked, the trailer creaked. Everywhere we dodged holes and

The top photo shows the north face of big and little Ararat which is located in Turkey near the Russian border. As a storm builds up over the summit, the south face of Mt. Ararat looks quite serene from a distance in the bottom photo. Neither view dampened the conquest spirits of Fernand and Raphael Navarra as they set out on their expedition to recover wood from Noah's Ark in 1955.

The top photo shows the Navarra family in 1955 near Karakose, the starting point where Navarra and his son Raphael made their historic climb to the summit of Mount Ararat. Pictured from left to right are Jose, 9; Raphael, 11; Mrs. Ascension Navarra and Fernand, age 13. In the bottom photograph Navarra and his son Raphael pose for a picture before departing for the mountain.

The area around Ararat on the lower elevations are occupied by a variety of nomadic people and shepherds. The life styles have not changed much during the past 2,000 years. The top photo shows homes in the "Valley of the Pigeons", which got its name from the number of pigeons in the area. Some birds are visible in the sky just above the uppermost cliff homes. In the numerous caves hermits have made their homes and left reminders such as these carved crosses on the walls.

Climbing Mt. Ararat was an extremely tiring adventure; eleven year old Raphael with his 40 pound back-pack needed to rest frequently. Navarra is seen resting at the side of Lac de Kop (Lake of the Summit) at an altitude of 3,850 meters. Lac de Kop became the base camp for the expedition because it was one of the few areas where fresh water existed in abundance.

Climbing Mt. Ararat is like scaling a gigantic pile of sand with rocks that slide under every step causing climbers to fall or stumble. Rocks sliding under climber's feet frequently cause landslides. In the photo Raphael is being assisted over the treacherous rocks by a rope cable attached to Fernand Navarra who is not pictured.

Mt. Ararat being a volcanic mountain is strewn with millions of rocks which even the shout of a human voice can cause a landslide and alter the appearance of the mountain on a daily basis, making it extremely difficult for climbing. More than once Navarra and his son narrowly escaped from huge boulders rolling down the mountainside. The photo shows a landslide in progress.

During the expedition, Navarra and his son used a pup tent braced up by two poles and their climbing axes. Although the tent was not very warm, it did serve as an excellent wind breaker. Most of the food cooked by Navarra on the expedition was done on a tablet camp stove. Food for the expedition consisted primarily of soups, juices, dried fruits, chocolates and tea.

Raphael climbs over the moraine strewn glacial ice pack en route to the exact location where the ark is encased. In the lower photo, Raphael rests atop the pup tent after it was demolished by a wind storm. Rocks frequently roll across the ice packs as did the one which came to a stop on the tent in this photo. The tent was not occupied when the rock collided with it. These rocks later become part of the ice pack and make digging efforts through ice packs extremely difficult.

open gutters. We inched around hairpin turns. And suddenly we thought we were in Alsace, an Alsace straight out of Hansi's picture-books. Here was the village of Feredjik, with a stork on each roof. Pleasant old men conversed on the cafe doorsteps, and they could speak French! Children as beautiful as Greek gods scuffled, naked, in the dust.

Shortly after we left Feredjik, the sky turned black and a gale blew up, covering us with dust. One of those Mediterranean storms broke over us, fortunately as brief as it was violent. But the road had turned to mud, and we had to cut reeds again to get our car out of the miry holes in the road.

We labored along till we reached Demotika, which we passed through without stopping, hoping to find better roads. But we still skidded along on a clay-covered trail while the gusty wind whisked far-blown dust into our faces. To make things worse, I braked suddenly to avoid a big rut and loosened the trunk fastenings. The luggage rack came crashing off the roof onto the hood of the car. We managed to repair the damage by nightfall.

We drove on a few hundred yards, then heard the sound of broken metal. We stopped and got out. The trailer tie had broken. We repaired it the best we could. Not too well, as it broke again farther on. This time we used a flat spring and a rope to make a splint.

By midnight we thought we were ready to go again, but now the starter would not respond. The battery was dead, and it was no help when the rain started again, heavier than ever.

We attempted to start the car by pushing it down a slope, but without success. We gave up, got out a tarpaulin, and lay down, but did not sleep much. The rain's patter stopped, but the crickets' chirping replaced it.

At sunrise, two of our men left for the closest village,

Yenikoy. Two hours later they came back by bus, carrying the battery of the only radio station in the area. Then they boarded the bus again, to get a mechanic from Demotika.

The trailer was gradually falling apart on the bad roads, but we finally reached Kastniais, the Greek border post, then the customs office at Edirne, on June 21.

iii

From Edirne onward, the road was excellent, and the following day we arrived in Istanbul.

This exotic city, drenched with bright sunlight, reminded us of Marseilles—only this city, with its busy port, with ships and boats of so many kinds, and its cosmopolitan sights, sounds, and smells, seemed to have colors more intense than the French city. The boats looked as if they had just been painted. On the Golden Horn, the caïques seemed to have just sailed in from a fairy tale.

We parked the car in the gardens of the French embassy. The cultural attaché received us pleasantly, but told us he doubted if we had much chance to enter the military zone. The last attempts made by other expeditions, he said, had been in vain. However, he advised us to go on to Ankara, where we would have a better chance than in Istanbul.

In Ankara, the ambassador, Mr. de Saint-Hardouin, greeted us amiably and arranged a meeting with the Minister of Tourism and the Minister of Home Affairs. These men offered us some hope, but told us we could not get permits in any event in less than three weeks.

"Why don't you visit Cappadocia while you're waiting?" the

Ministry of Tourism advised us. "This region is almost unknown, and I don't think anyone has filmed it in color."

It was a good idea, we agreed, and on July 9 we left for that part of Turkey. The next day we camped in old Urgup, or Cappadocia. We were to stay there ten days, during which our cameramen traveled around.

Cappadocia presented a striking contrast to the harsh, colorless steppe of Central Anatolia. White cliffs barred the skyline, tinged, depending on the time of the day, with yellow, pink, or tender blue. Throughout the green countryside stood pyramids and cones, the highest of which reached 3,250 feet. Some of them were topped with rocks. This was the Valley of a Thousand Churches.

From a distance, it looked like thousands of spires, steeples, and pinnacles. These sharp rocks, probably of volcanic origin, had been hollowed out, sometimes until almost empty. Depending on their size, they had one or more rooms, each with window openings. Who hollowed out these dwellings? The monks and hermits who lived there until the Ottoman invasion were only the last of a succession of occupants.

In Cappadocia, formerly one of the centers of Christianity in Asia Minor, we viewed numerous architectural ruins. We saw rupestral (carved out of the rock) churches decorated with frescoes, the most ancient of which were related to Syriano-Palestinian art. Others showed a Byzantine influence, witnessing to the extension of that culture toward the East. In return, in the fourteenth century, Byzantium absorbed Oriental influences transmitted through Cappadocia. Thus the region became a melting pot for the various elements which formed the Byzantine art.

Other surprises awaited us. Several Urgup inhabitants distinctly resembled the Basques of France and Spain. Their cooking was similar to that of the provinces of Provence and Languedoc, especially when they prepared a *turlu firin,* a dish made of eggplant, cucumber, and tomato. On the Mediterranean coast, this is called a *drapeau* (flag). To top things off, the vines, terraced on the heights, planted in straight lines and pruned in a tumbler shape, also reminded us of southern France.

On July 22, we were back in Ankara chafing to move on to Ararat. We had applied for permits through Dr. Halim Alyot, press officer, and Colonel Hakki Atil, head of Army Propaganda. But we needed approval of three different governmental departments and the Army special services as well. Travelers know what that means, in any country in the world.

The days passed. From time to time, we were encouraged. "This time you're all set. Everything is fine," they would say. Then the next day, we suspected that the officials, for all their politeness, were preparing a refusal.

We wondered if the waiting in offices would ever have an end. The heat stifled us in spite of ventilators. On July 30, we could wait no longer. We had lost hope. We had succeeded in making ourselves known in Ankara, but this seemed to work against us. It took away our last chance, that of entering the forbidden zone secretly. We prepared to pack up and go home.

On July 31, as we discussed our homeward route, Colonel Hakki Atil summoned us and gave us a tiny paper, duly signed. It was a permit to climb Mount Ararat! The decision, he said, had been made July 24!

We leaped for joy. Suddenly we neither felt the oppressive heat nor cared about the 800 miles that still separated us from Mount Ararat. A negligible run!

With new optimism, we departed, but only three of us. The

authorization had a stipulation attached: we were also to film the Ephesus pilgrimage taking place at that time.

On August 3, the three of us headed for Mount Ararat, leaving Raymond Zerbini and Michel Vailland to travel to Ephesus. Our first goal was Erzerum. There we would contact the army to plan the ascent of the mountain with them. Another condition they imposed in granting our permit was that we would film an army battalion climbing Ararat.

From Ankara to Erzerum, the countryside changed according to altitude: wooded slopes, meadows, narrow valleys, streams, and brooks lined with poplar trees and willows. Then the valleys became deeper, grooved with streams and yellow-orange sandbanks. We saw villages of puddled clay houses. At 6,500 feet we came to the first mountain pass, where an expanse of eastern Turkey spread before us like a huge congealed sea. Like stormy waves, mountain ranges seemed to clash against each other in confused disarray. The spectrum of colors ranged from the night-blue of the skyline and the green of the summits through ochre, mauve, and gold. The temperature changed constantly. From the stifling heat of the valleys, we passed to chilling cold on the heights, which forced us to exchange our colonial helmets for furred bonnets and to put on our ski jackets. In the altitudes, the steering wheel was ice-cold. In the valleys, we again felt the heat.

When we were hungry, we stopped in the villages and ate yogurt and shishkebab—after we had shooed off the flies.

iv

We had been told that Erzerum was a city of 60,000 inhabitants. When we arrived, it seemed more like a big village, and we wondered how it could hold that many people.

After cleaning up, we reported at the fort. We showed our pass, and immediately the soldiers let us through the door into an inner court. There we found a gate guarded by other armed soldiers. Near the gate stood a guardian's tent with a young officer at the threshold. Gathering our meager Turkish vocabulary, we addressed him first.

To our great surprise, he introduced himself in French.

"Lieutenant Ozdemir Tokay. My father was a diplomat and could speak French. I intend to be one myself, and I have been brought up by a French governess."

Our contacts with military authorities were off to a good start. Ozdemir took us to the police station, where they had been expecting us. But our files had not arrived yet, and we would have to wait for them. We were hardly pleased with this prospect, but Ozdemir took us to the commanding officer charged with organizing our expedition.

We explained our plans. First, we wished to penetrate as far as possible into the valley of Ahora, the village destroyed in the 1840 earthquake. Next we wanted to climb Mount Ararat, and finally we hoped to discover the lake in which, according to many witnesses, the Ark is partly submerged.

With the aid of our maps, we planned our itinerary: Bayazid, Igdir, Ahora, and, if need be, Sardarbulak in the East. The commanding officer agreed fully. In Bayazid, we would stay at the Officers' Club. The colonel commanding the area would take us to the Igdir Club for the night, and the next day would furnish us with a guide to reach Ahora. From there, we would leave to explore the valley. In the meantime, we would be the guests of the Erzerum Officers' Club. Their hospitality could not have been greater. As we expressed our thanks, the commanding officer interrupted to ask Ozdemir if he wanted to accompany us. The lieutenant accepted, blushing with pleasure.

On the morning of August 7, our file arrived at the police headquarters. Once this was checked, we were ready at last to head eastward. Our team had been strengthened by two choice additions, Lieutenant Ozdemir Tokay and our friend Alaedin Seker, official motion-picture photographer for the Turkish Propaganda and Tourism Office. The road to Mount Ararat opened ahead of us.

We made our first halt, to eat lunch, at Hasankale. This town lay at the foot of a cliff crowned by a Seljoukian fortress, in ruins but still proud. In front of us lay a trickle of water, the headwaters of the Aras River. The stream would be with us all the way to Mount Ararat before it flowed into the Caspian Sea. Along its banks, two hot-water springs had given birth to a famous *hammam,* or Turkish bathhouse. There were two identical buildings, one for women and one for men.

"Wealthy customers come here to relax," Ozdemir told us. "The treatment starts with a steam bath, and after a good sweat, a massage on a tiled table. Then the patient, washed, rinsed, and bruised, can go back to his excesses of *raki* drinking and good eating."

Ozdemir knew the region well. He showed us an old bridge spanning the river Aras. "Notice," he said, "the little Romanesque niche. After the Sultan had the bridge built, he had the workmen set a small jewel box of emeralds into the masonry to pay for future repairs of the bridge. The bridge has held up, but bandits long ago stole the emeralds."

Next we halted at Horassan, where we were happy to find a gasoline pump. It seemed that the whole population gathered around us here. They had learned of our trip from the newspaper. Women talked vehemently as they gesticulated toward us. Our Turkish host told us they were saying we would never reach the top of Mount Ararat. No one had ever reached it, not even Dr. Smith, whom everybody there remembered.

We would see. An officer insisted, so the gatekeeper let us by, and we started up the Tahir Gorges. The road along the ledge had been washed out and never repaired. A creek ran down below, and above us stones fell from the crumbly cliffs. We felt we didn't want to stay there long. "This place is bad enough," Ozdemir told us, "but besides its natural dangers, it's a favorite hideout for bandits. There have been many ambushes along this historical route between the Ports of the Levant—Trabzon, Bayburt, Erzerum, Karakose, Bayazid—and the Caspian Sea."

The sun had disappeared, and the low sky had taken the mauve tint of the neighboring mountains. We saw before us a wide, high plateau on which lay the town of Karakose, now called Agri. From Karakose we had hoped to see Mount Ararat, but now night had come. We checked into the Transit Hotel, a caravansary divided into rooms furnished with four to six beds each. Several of these bedrooms, if they could be called bedrooms, had been taken by the passengers of an old bus we had seen just before we arrived. On the upper deck of the bus, we saw several people tied down.

"Are they prisoners?" we asked.

"No, they are travelers," Ozdemir had explained. "They are fastened so they won't fall off in the turns, and also to keep them from running away when the bus stops, before they have paid!"

We were so tired that we slept in spite of the uncomfortable beds and the screams of the child of one of the travelers. In the morning, we had the gas tank filled, and left. The day was already hot, with a dust-laden wind blowing. The dazzling sun hurt our eyes, so that we had a dual reason for tears in our eyes when the Mountain of the Deluge finally came in view.

There it was, hazy in the light, tinted with mauve, distinct from the sky only because of its cap of ice. It looked as unreal as a Japanese print. As if to make sure this was no mirage, we stopped the car, got out, and adjusted our telescope on its tripod. Squinting through the eyepiece, we could see, near the top, the terrace various climbers had described, where the Ark might have run aground. We saw the large névés* caught between the rocky ridges, which seemed to support the mountain like the flying buttresses of a cathedral.

The remaining miles to Bayazid we covered as fast as the road would allow.

Bayazid—the new Bayazid—was built up on both sides of the road. The old city, 5,000 feet high, to the southwest of the mountain, used to lie to one side of the road to Iran. A deep, narrow gully separated it from the Persian district on the steep slope.

The governor and a colonel in command of the town received us in Turkish style, with sweets and tea. Then they suggested that we reconnoiter the Iranian border post. Again we jogged eastward through the dust, the colonel riding with us. As we drew closer, the two Ararats appeared in all their majesty. They seemed like gigantic Siamese twins, held by the saddle of the Sardarbulak pass, point of departure for so many explorers moved by faith and hope similar to ours.

"This pass," the colonel told us, "is only 7,500 feet high. You can get there on horseback. At this season, there are good

---

* Compacted snow at the upper end of a glacier.

pastures, and since there is water, it is the best starting point to reach the summit of either Ararat."

But we intended to attack the giant neither from Sardarbulak nor from Bayazid. Why follow beaten paths if the ark had not been discovered that way? Long before, we had decided on our route. We would explore the northern, western, and southwestern sides before attempting the big climb.

Old Bayazid, however, was well worth a visit. The Sultans' city slept in tragic solitude. On a rock stood the mosque, in elegant pink and gold. From its balcony, every spring, a young virgin had been hurled to insure the gods' protection. The mosque and the palace were built in 1186. Fifty-two thousand men worked on them for thirty years. Every stone of the wall, decorated with stylized flowers and animals, showed a Persian influence.

We entered through the monumental door of the fortress, descended fifteen marble steps, and found ourselves before the tombs of Isaac Pasha and his favorite wife. The golden jewelry, precious stones, embroideries, and brocades had been stolen long before. The bronze door of the mosque and the bronze rings around the base of the white marble pillars had also been removed. Only the wonderful frescoes remained.

We strolled through the empty throne room, harem, children's apartments, reception rooms, guards' rooms, and kitchens. In these, we saw traces of soot in the huge fireplaces. Our camera operator filmed this rather forlorn reminder of a grandiose past. Then we left for Ahora.

v
___

The outpost Ahora lay slightly northeast, at the foot of Noah's mountain. We avoided the east side by going around Little Ararat. We also avoided Sardarbulak Pass, impossible to negotiate with a car. We took the westward road which, through Cencel Cedigi Pass, between Mount Aghri-Dagh (Ararat) and Mount Hama-Da, led us into the Aras Valley, to Agdir. From there we continued to Aralik Baskow, and finally along the mule path to the outpost Ahora, where they say Noah planted the first vine.

Out of Bayazid, the road followed a narrow plain of volcanic ashes and sterile sand, infernally hot, a region where nothing could grow and no one could live. Only a few dwarfed shrubs, with little foliage, bristled with thorns. We drove along the first foothills of the southern and western sides of Mount Ararat, whose basaltic rocks stood out, jagged, like needles and organ pipes, purple and ash-blue. From a distance, the biblical mountain had appeared uniform and even around its base. From close up, details began to take shape.

We kept turning until we reached a low spot where reeds grew. Here and there, grooves lined the lava, letting the water run off intermittently. Sometimes the water disappeared altogether. We stopped, opened our map, aimed the telescope, and examined the terrain: 6,250 square miles, at least two-thirds of it occupied by Great Ararat. We would have to divide this enormous surface into sectors and methodically explore each sector.

Now the trail climbed up through fields of pink and yellow flowers. We were approaching the medium zone, where the first clouds disappeared. Then, influenced by the moraines and the glaciers, the clouds rested heavily on this pasture area. Every night we could see the clouds take shape, hide the cap, and disappear during the night. Strange phenomenon, resulting from the extreme temperature differences between the base and the summit.

We drove through Cencel Cedigi Pass. The sun had disappeared, and the icy air obliged us to put on our ski jackets. As we descended, the temperature became milder, and we arrived at Igdir in a stifling night without the slightest breeze. Still following the Aras River, we reached the Turko-Russian border near Erivan and Nakitchevan, Noah's first home and landing place, according to tradition. The ground in Igdir was made of sand and ashes, but eucalyptus, birch, plane, and even pear trees grew there. We had a meal at the Officers' Club, then went to bed.

The following morning at seven o'clock we left for Ahora under an already burning sun. The trail followed the Aras River and crossed dried streams and crevasses. Those forty-five uneven miles reminded us of Greek roads.

At noon we entered Aralik, an army post only 2,500 feet above sea level. From there to the top of Ararat we had 14,500 feet to climb.

The first 3,000 feet we drove through a desert area of sand and ashes with clusters of juniper trees here and there. Then the scenery changed. Blocks of lava, sometimes four or five yards high, dotted the ashy ground. Beyond, we found fields of volcanic boulders, of trachytic rocks, of dolerites baking in the sun. At 5,000 feet we came to a muddy stream, and in spite of its uninviting appearance, we had a long drink. When we wanted to leave, the car engine stalled and stopped. We had to walk the rest of the way—500 yards.

A police captain, head of the post in Ahora, came to meet us. Five minutes later we were sitting at a table under a screen of reeds, doing justice to a delicious meal. As we ate our dessert, a shepherd arrived. He was Yusuf Tozu, son of chief Hassan Tozu, a "lord" in the area. He told us he had been a friend of Colonel Lawrence, and used to help him stir up revolt against the Turks. Nowadays, Yusuf helped the police captain maintain order in the area.

The village of Ahora was slowly reviving. Where twelve years ago all had lain in ruins, the village now had 300 people who raised livestock and farmed. This was a real oasis, well irrigated—a pleasant spot to live.

News traveled fast in Ararat country. Yusuf already knew of our plans and offered to lead us along the right-hand side of the valley, which followed the moraine.

We walked with him along the grassy hills where sheep grazed here and there. Above us stood a cliff, with a series of caves. Yusuf pointed one cave out to us:

"That is where, some time ago, my father hid Colonel Lawrence for more than a month. I was just a child, and sometimes at nightfall I would take him wheat cakes and yogurt."

We entered the cave. Looking back, we saw that the cave's opening framed Mount Ararat. One would like to know the mystic adventurer's thoughts as he gazed at the biblical mountain. Before him, monks had lived in these caves, getting their food from offerings the shepherds brought. We noticed templars' crosses engraved on the walls. For centuries, this valley had been a refuge for hermits. Now these cracks in the rocks sheltered only pigeons, and cattle when stormy rains beat down.

We climbed up farther to the moraine front, 7,375 feet high, before the approaching night compelled us to return to our Ahora camp.

On August 10, at five in the morning, our caravan started. The police captain led the way on horseback. Yusuf accompanied us, and several herdsmen chiefs joined him. There were twenty of us.

After exploring the right-hand side of the valley the day before, now we explored the left side. The rules of hospitality slowed our progress; after an hour we had to stop in a shepherds' camp. They offered us tea and mutton. We said we could not eat meat so early, but how could we rudely slight their hospitality? I decided to amuse them, thus winning their friendship without eating the food I did not want. I turned some somersaults and did handstands on two mountain goat horns planted in the ground. After that, the shepherds quit urging us to eat and let us go.

A narrow path barred with fallen rocks led us above the moraine, and we finally arrived at the sacred fountain of Saint Jacob, whose legend the captain related to us.

"One day the prophet Jacob wanted to make a pilgrimage to the Ark with a few companions," he began. "As the pilgrims, dying of thirst, could not walk any further, Jacob hit the ground with his heel and a clear spring burst forth. He called to those behind, 'Aghri! Aghri!' (Come!) Thus one of the Turkish names for Mount Ararat originated: Aghri Dagh. 'Dagh' means mountain. The pilgrims, their thirst quenched, recovered their strength and climbed on upward to Noah's vessel."

"Which way did they go?" we asked.

A shepherd showed us a breach in the right-hand wall, on the other slope toward the southwest.

"This way, but it is not possible to go there. There is *magic spell!*"

The other shepherds nodded. A fearful silence came over the group as we contemplated the site of Ahora, the village engulfed, with all its inhabitants, by the earthquake of 1840. Only one wild rosebush, with knotted ribbons tied on it, remained to mark the spot. Saint Jacob's fountain, fed by a spring, was still a place of pilgrimage, and the ribbons were the pilgrims' votive offerings. According to tradition, they had to cut a ribbon from their clothing, attach it to a branch of the rosebush, and make a wish. The wish would come true within the year. Afterward, they could drink from the spring.

We observed the rite, then pushed on forward. The valley narrowed and the ridges grew steeper. The captain had to dismount. With some trouble, we reached the moraine, whose sloping sides ended in gullies. To our surprise, the stream that lower down had flowed in the left-hand gully now flowed in the right-hand one.

Yusuf explained: "The ancients talked of huge 'cellars' where the water got lost, then reappeared in unexpected places."

Other mountains share this phenomenon, but Ararat's stream is peculiar in that it comes out muddier than it goes in. Almost all of the water on Ararat comes from thawing ice and snow, and is muddy. The nomads drink it, beaten with yogurt in large basins; they call it *aynan.* Only the water from the Saint Jacob fountain, which was spring water, was clear. One of the shepherds told us that one month before the disaster, the spring had stopped flowing. This was an omen for these simple people,

27

and for us a sign that the volcano must be still internally active.

We still climbed under an implacable sun whose heat the rocks reflected. One of the shepherds screamed, and at once an avalanche started, stopping only at the foot of the moraine. We were traveling on a flat stretch where there was no danger to us, but we were so taken by surprise that we did not get any pictures of the avalanche.

The captain smiled. "These rock slides can be provoked at will. Just shout when you want one."

We screamed again, and a dusty smoke rose from the corridor of fallen debris, followed by an impressive avalanche. This time our cameraman had only to aim.

At eleven, we shared our crackers, chocolate, and malt with the shepherds, who were delighted with this picnic meal. But when we wanted to resume the climb, they looked at each other and refused to go farther. Yusuf was the only one to keep on, in spite of the "spell."

At 10,000 feet, real difficulties began. Roped together, we crossed the foot of the glacier, made of piles of mixed earth and ice. Strangely, a pond between the glacier and the rocky wall gave forth bubbles of sulfurous gas. Around it we saw a quantity of small, regular cones, three to four feet high, made of black ashes and red-orange earth. The ground was a mixture of ash tuffs, volcanic muds, and deposits of black coal dust. A mountain stream strewn with shiny blocks of lava attracted the attention of our camera operators.

As we moved forward on the glacier, the crevasses became wider and their edges more vertical. Some of them were five or six yards wide. We leaned forward, one after the other, roped together, to try to estimate their depth, but without success. We weighted a rope with a block of lava and reeled out thirty yards of it without touching the bottom which was hidden in shadows. We lost time skirting these abysses. Finally we found a "chimney" through which we climbed up to 11,500 feet. Grouped there on a platform, we could see the breach the shepherds had pointed out before, the breach through which Saint Jacob and his companions had arrived at the Ark. We would not mind going that way ourselves, in spite of the stiff climb to 13,000 feet, but we had made no preparations to camp at night. Evening was coming, and as the shadows lengthened toward the valley, it was time to go back. We had proved only one thing—that the legend about the "spell" was false, for nothing supernatural had stopped us. And when we heard two shots, it was only a signal from the captain urging us to go back. This we did, laboriously.

At the second shepherds' camp, the lamb we had refused in the morning sizzled on an iron sheet. This time we didn't need urging.

In the distance, Erivan shone with a thousand lights. We thought we would like to visit that city until we learned that in August the temperature varies from 110° to 120° Fahrenheit in the shade and that one can cook eggs in the sand. From 10:00 A.M. until 5:00 P.M., few of its citizens venture into the streets because of the intense heat.

They have a local saying, "Cold in winter and hot in summer—in Erivan the living are no better off than the dead."

vi

We left again from Bayazid on August 12 for the ascent of the southern side. In 120-degree heat, we crossed the pebbly plain to the first foothills of Mount Ararat, where the tents of the base camp appeared.

Clouds of mosquitoes surrounded us, and they swarmed around the naked chests of the soldiers waiting for the colonel to pass the review. The colonel arrived late, at 11:00 A.M., and the review lasted half an hour. The stoical soldiers, led by a pleasant young lieutenant, Sehap Atalay, neither fidgeted nor complained about the burning sun or the mosquitoes. We were not so brave, and took shelter under the tents. By three that afternoon, thick black clouds piled up, obscuring the sun. Sensing the promise of rain, all the insects of the plain had come out of their holes—grasshoppers, giant crickets, praying mantises, huge ants, weevils, and beetles.

Slightly before six, the pack-mules lent us by the army arrived to carry our equipment. Immediately afterward, a flash of lightning from the direction of Mount Ararat ripped the clouds. As if on a divine signal, the whole sky blazed. The great glacier flashed and seemed to flow along the slopes like melted glass. Then came a deluge, which seemed quite appropriate and biblical to us. Though wet through, our tent held up well in spite of the gusts that shook it and filled it like a balloon. We sheltered our equipment under tarpaulins and stood near the center pole.

The storm died down after nearly three hours, the night grew cooler, and the mosquitoes attacked us again. We watched the stars twinkle in a marvelously clear sky. We arose at five, having slept very little.

Once the mules were loaded, we climbed up through the first pastures—8,000 feet, 9,000 feet. Following a goat trail, we edged along a gully, Little Ararat to our right. When we reached 9,800 feet, we thought we stood as high as its summit, yet it still towered 2,950 feet higher than we. Tall green grass partially hid the blocks of lava here.

On the southern slope, at 12,450 feet, we came to the camp of Hazam Calatin, a mountain prince about forty years of age. He greeted us and invited us to a feast of tea, boiled chickens, wheat cakes, sheep, and goat cheeses. The women of the tribe, in multicolored dresses, obligingly posed for our cameras. We ate with the tips of our fingers, in accordance with local custom. While we were sheltered under their goat-hair tents, the rain returned, bringing hail with it.

An hour and a half later, good weather returned, and we went on, Hazam Calatin leading the way. He walked like a mountaineer, knees bent, and head forward. He had already reconnoitered the terrain up to a rocky ridge which should, he said, lead us quickly to the top. For almost four hours we followed Hazam through névés and pastures, for the latter extended high up the mountain on the southern side. Fortunately, the mosquitoes had left us alone, but clouds, with intermittent showers and hail up to 13,450 feet, hindered our progress, and we had to climb over and around numerous blocks of lava.

At six o'clock, we decided it would be foolish to try to go farther. Hazam took us to the spot he had chosen to set up our No. 2 camp, on a bumpy plateau covered with erratic blocks, but with enough open surface to set up the tents. We had just put these up when a snowstorm started, a blizzard which covered the blue basalt with white. At the same moment, our mules and their drivers arrived equally tired. The mules had suffered, and so had their packs; every case had been dented or ripped. Milk, jam, chocolate, alcohol fuel, made a horrible mixture. We succeeded in preparing cocoa, which was not quite

what it should have been, but at least was hot. Afterward we
went to sleep, listening to the snow-muffled night noises. Next
day we hoped to reach our goal.

Before dawn, August 14, we arose and left the tent. A strong,
icy wind whipped our faces. Leaden clouds, heavy with snow,
were gathering. The snow that had fallen during the night
sounded wet underfoot, and our footprints filled with water
which froze quickly.

We shared the loads—boxes of film, food supplies, first-aid
kits, pitons, binoculars, cameras, ropes, and pickaxes.

Hazam Calatin walked in front. He had chosen a path
between two névés, a sharp ridge strewn with boulders.
Between them, uneven stones covered the ground. Moving
forward was difficult. We had to scale the blocks, and the slope
was steep. After this chaos, the ridge grew even sharper, with
sharp rocks on which we cut ourselves when we fell. Mount
Ararat is a volcano, whose rocks are lava, basalts, and trachytes,
now in ridges, now in organ pipes or huge blocks.

At 9:00 A.M., we reached 15,400 feet. A half hour later, the
altimeter read 15,850 feet, and we still felt quite fit. Here,
Hazam Calatin took advantage of a halt to announce that he
would not go farther. He could still climb, he said, but he did
not want to break the unwritten law which lays some kind of
curse on the summit. We had to let him go.

The more I saw of Lieutenant Sehap Atalay, the more I
admired him. He led us all, getting ahead, stopping, watching us
climb. His eyes were clear, sharp, protective. Thanks to him, we
reached the summit that day.

We stood at the angle of two large névés which we were to
follow up to a terrace from where we could see the cap.

Through an opening of the clouds, we glimpsed Bayazid—Bayazid aflame while we shivered.

It was not good at such a height to make prolonged halts. We realized this when we set forth again. Our cooled joints rebelled when we started to move again. Breathing was difficult. The rarified air, the lower pressure, made us gasp. We had the feeling that the mountain was defending itself. Just lifting an arm was painful, and throwing the pickaxe forward to catch a block seemed impossible. We wanted to lie down and sleep and put an end to following these stations of the cross, with frequent falls.

It took us over four hours to climb 300 yards. Under our feet, nothing was solid, neither rocks nor ice. Everything rolled and fell apart. We were not walking, but clawing, our bodies stuck to the ground, trying to adhere to the moving wall.

Bruised, with scum on our lips, we finally reached a terrace of hard ice. We broke off pieces which we sucked, hoping to quench our thirst, but this ice did not melt, and worse yet, it was salty. And the terrace was not the last one before the top, as we had thought. Mount Ararat is like that: after a terrace which hides the cap, another one comes, which hides the following one, and so on.

We progressed anyway, twenty or thirty steps in succession, then a halt. A sharp wind kept us awake. Above our heads, a cover of dark clouds gathered; underneath us, a sea of lighter clouds. Between the two, as between two shrouds, we were rowing in a moonlike scene, hallucinating, wondering if we were losing our minds. Was this the origin of the "curse"? "There is a magic spell," they had told us. Men had come this far in former times, mountain sickness had taken hold of them, and in their simple minds, they had ascribed this phenomenon to the deity. Hazam Calatin had known what awaited us.

A large seam of ice hid the Turkish soldiers who were with us. We crawled forward on hands and feet, one pulling the other. The big seam changed into a crevassed wall. Our roped group was like a ship in distress when we reached a promontory of compact ice from whence we could see the cap, six or seven hundred yards to the northwest. Nothing else lay beyond.

The altimeter read 16,934 feet. A few steps more and we would touch the summit of Noah's mountain, "Mother of the World"!

vii

We had fulfilled the first part of our goal—to climb the mountain. Now the historical part—the most important part to me—remained. Now I wanted to find the remains of the Ark. A heavy snowstorm hindered our descent, but we succeeded in reaching camp No. 2 at dusk, and the following day arrived back in Bayazid.

Now we wanted to explore the west side of the mountain, the side on which the Etchmiadzin monks turned their telescope to show Noah's vessel to travelers. On that side, Kop Lake (Kip-Choll Lake) was located, the lake above which Frederic Parrot set up camp in September, 1829, on his third expedition. Our first goal would be to reconnoiter Lake Kop.

On August 16, at 6:00 A.M., we left Igdir for Baskow, then took the Ahora trail. As soon as we reached 3,600 feet, we made our first discovery. We were very near the western face. The cap of Mount Ararat, with the sun behind it, outlined a bright, transparent fringe. All of a sudden, we shouted, "The Ark!"

Two-thirds of the way up the mountain, its bow stood out, black on a background of light-colored rocks. But, when we came closer, we found that this bow was only a spur of rock, the same one the monks pointed out from their monastery, without ever having climbed up to verify what it was. We had not discovered the real thing yet, but we had put an end to a legend.

We had climbed only a few hundred feet above the bow spur when a rock under our feet started to come loose. The two of us remained hanging on a platform of a few square feet. The rock rolled, pulling off other rocks, descending to the foot of the cliff and beyond. A close call!

At last we set foot on the moraine made of lava dust, volcanic ashes, and rocky debris. Slipping and sliding, we reached a harder, more compact strip which gave access to a pile of stones. On our right, a large empty gully yawned; on our left, the beginning of the glacier. Farther down the slope, the bow-shaped spur and beyond, fallen rocks and ice in a half circle, barred the whole valley. Above, we could see the huge cap of the summit.

We were above the Ahora breach, opened along a depression which marked the division of the glaciers. Those on the right went down toward Ahora, those on the left flowed into the northwest glacier.

Nothing here revealed the presence of the Ark. We must go farther up. All of a sudden we heard a thunderous roar, which echoed around the mountain. From down in the valley a mist rose, a cloud of white dust twirling beneath us. A formidable rumble shook the whole mountain. It was the working of the seracs,* the noisy march of the glaciers.

Just as the echoes died down, four bears appeared a hundred yards from us. We had been warned that bears lived on Mount Ararat, but we were unarmed, and we had no way to retreat from them. To keep our visitors at a respectful distance, we had only a pickaxe.

But the bears seemed to have only the best of intentions. They played together, rolling around and teasing each other. The two older ones, probably the mother and father, started sniffing around, then went back toward the summit, followed by the young ones.

On August 17, at two in the afternoon, I was alone on the cap of ice, which in this place was clear of snow. I felt no fatigue, but a great anxiety. In the sky, an eagle circled, carried by the wind.

I crossed an arm of the glacier and climbed to the top of the moraine. On one side, I could see a mountain of ice lined with crevasses, on the other, a sheer wall. At the bottom, I saw a dark mass.

This mass was clearly outlined, its lines straight and curved, and approximately 120 yards long. The general shape, I thought, resembled that of a ship.

I had never had hallucinations. My mind was perfectly clear, and those who knew me had usually given me credit for having common sense.

At that altitude, in that desert of ice, what could it be? The ruins of a building, church, refuge, or house never mentioned in

---

* Seracs are ice pinnacles or blocks into which a glacier breaks on a steep slope.

any account, any tradition, never seen by any of those who came to this place? The wreckage of an airplane? No one ever used beams of that size to build a fuselage.

Those remains, I thought, must be what's left of the Ark. Perhaps this is the flat bottom of the biblical vessel, the top structures of which must have been scattered. Didn't Berose say that in his time the people pulled off fragments of the Ark to scrape the asphalt coating?

The structure was really there, but out of reach, and I lacked the necessary equipment to go down to the site. All I could do was to locate as accurately as possible the site of my discovery and rejoin my companions, promising myself that I would come back again.

CHAPTER 3

Second Expedition—1953

Our expedition had been a success from an alpinist's point of view, for we had scaled the fabled mountain. But as regards the discovery of the Ark, it was an apparent failure. We brought back neither fragment nor photograph.

In my press release, I could not mention my discovery of August 17. If when they asked, "Have you seen the Ark?" I had answered, "No, but I know where it is," people would have accused me of lying. I could only keep silent and plan for another trip to the mountain.

In July 1953, I made a second attempt, accompanied by a Turkish photographer. I found my way fairly easily, climbing to within a hundred yards of the site of the timbers. But boulders, perched precariously above, rolled down at the sound of my voice. Photographer Alaedin Seker had already stopped his climb, and I was on my own.

I was able to get about twenty yards closer, when I suddenly felt faint. My head felt as if it was caught in a vise and about to burst. I could not coordinate my movements, and could think of only one thing—to go back down! I sat down and shut my eyes. For ten minutes, I felt numb. I left and, twenty yards lower, found my companion, pale, curled up between two rocks, visibly as bad off as I was. I warmed him up and cheered him as well as I could, but we were both so exhausted that during the three hours of our descent to camp, we did not utter a word.

The success of the lectures I gave upon my return, particularly at the Palais de Chaillot, showed me that people's interest in the search for the Ark had not died down in spite of our failures.

My own interest kept on growing, becoming an obsession. Night and day, I recalled the dusty Turkish roads, the glaciers, the moraines of disintegrated rocks, and the big shadow of the Ark. At night, I dreamed of extraordinary ways by which I could pull off a fragment of the wreck and triumphantly bring it back.

Months went by. In September, 1954, I learned that the American, John Libi, had come within thirty yards of the Ark, and that he planned another expedition in 1955. Then I made up my mind: I would go a third time.

The Libi story reinforced my conviction that the glaciers had receded. What had not been possible in 1952 and 1953 might be possible in 1955. If the winter was mild, my chances of reaching the Ark would be better.

CHAPTER 4

Third Expedition—1955

i

To explore Mount Ararat, a forbidden military zone, I needed to obtain a pass which the Turkish authorities were reluctant to give. To apply before I left France was to be refused, most likely. To journey to Turkey and request the permit there, as we had done in 1952, was to risk being told every day for a month or two: "Come back tomorrow." And I had no time to lose.

My knowledge of the area enabled me to plan an itinerary along Lake Van, avoiding the main roads which are more closely watched. But even after having taken this precaution, I might meet up with a police patrol. Any foreigner in a border area is suspected of spying. However, a family on vacation would hardly arouse suspicion. That is why I decided to take my wife and three sons, Fernand, thirteen, Raphael, eleven, and Jose, nine.

We set our departure for June, 1955. We planned to go to Beirut by boat, through Syria to the Turkish border, and up to Lake Van. Then we would join the international highway going from Istanbul to Iran, which runs by the foot of Mount Ararat.

In the meantime, we had eight months to practice. We began with the big sand dune at Le Pyla, near Arcachon, France, and later ascended Peak Vignemale in the Pyrenees. We climbed to about 8,900 feet. This experience enabled me to make a selection within my family. Jose was too young, and Fernand (Coco) seemed to have "growing pains," and would not be able to climb Mount Ararat. Raphael would come with me.

ii

On June 21, 1955, we left Bordeaux by car for Marseilles. We took walking shoes, mountain shoes, crampons, a tent, sleeping bags, gas and alcohol stoves, ladders, ropes, pickaxes, hatchets, two movie cameras, and four still ones.

On June 22, we boarded the *Malek Fouad*, of the Egyptian *Kedevial Mail Line*. We called at Genoa and Naples, visited Pompei, and arrived in Beirut on the 28th. The customs officers, more suspicious than their colleagues in Marseilles, searched our car inside and out.

That evening, we arrived in Zhale to spend the night. It is an old town famed for its cool springs. When I had stayed there eighteen years before, it had boasted four or five restaurants. Now it was a favorite summer resort for the Lebanese, with at least a hundred restaurants and several first-class hotels.

The next day, we went through Rayak, then through Balbek, the ancient Heliopolis, with its remarkable ruins. On the 30th, we arrived in Alep, where I called on the Turkish consul. I explained that I was on vacation with my family, and that I intended to go to Lake Van, Queen Semiramis' summer dwelling.

The consul showed no surprise, but gave me the same explanations as I had already heard a hundred times: the lake area was forbidden by the military authorities. He even advised me not to travel in his country. At last he produced a map of Turkey on which he outlined the limits within which I could travel freely. That meant the Mediterranean coast as far inland as Kayseri. Eastern Turkey was forbidden. He gave me the map.

I thanked the consul, and after having waited an hour and a half under a torrid afternoon sun, we crossed the Turkish border.

The passport officer did not speak a word of French. He sent for an interpreter, to whom I explained that we were going to Kayseri, then to Ankara. The officer then gave each of us a special form, which we were supposed to have stamped in all the hotels where we would stay; thus the authorities would be kept informed of our moves.

New complications lay ahead of us, but we were too tired to think about anything but food and rest. A customs officer told us about a "palace" that served meals in Soocluk, a mountain village 3,600 feet above Alexandrette (Iskanderum). There we had some of the best food of our whole stay in Turkey.

That evening we decided that my wife would stay, with Fernand and Jose, in a town on the Mediterranean coast, while I left for Mount Ararat with Raphael. This was a big change in our plans. Instead of five, only two of us would face the hardships and dangers of the ascent.

But in the morning my wife told me, "I have thought it over. If there is any risk, it is better for us all to be together. We shall be in the hands of God. We shall only leave you at the foot of Mount Ararat."

I agreed at once, glad to keep our family team together.

We studied the map the consul had given us, with some mistrust. My first expedition had taught me, among other things, that Turkish maps could not be relied on. In 1952 we had been told, on our way back, about a "very good road" which would gain us one day. I still remember the trail that had ruined our tires.

I decided to avoid Urfa, an army center, and take a main road to Elazig. There we would turn off to go by Lake Van. Then we would be only about sixty miles from Mount Ararat.

Everything went well as far as Maras. The paved road passed through wide cotton fields. This part of Turkey is rich; we only had trouble finding such items as sugar and, mainly, gas. In Maras, thirty miles inside the forbidden zone, three plainclothesmen in a jeep stopped us, asked to see our passports, and wanted to know where we were going.

I answered in Turkish that we were looking for a place to have lunch. They accepted this answer so well that they showed us to a restaurant. I invited one of them to eat with us, and he accepted readily. Onlookers crowded around our table, almost smothering us. The policeman sent them off rudely.

A little old man who spoke French, who said he had lived five years in Marseilles, appeared. The policeman, using him as an interpreter, asked what the goal of our journey was. My answer satisfied him, because he supplied us with gas, and we were off.

We drove on toward Elazig on a fairly good, though dusty, road. Before the sun set, we bought fruit, tomatoes, and meat.

43

Buying meat at that season, in that part of the world, involves incessant brushing off flies, and all five of us got busy shooing the insects. Of course, the meat is mutton. From the sheep hanging on a hook, the butcher slices off a boneless strip, which he pounds vigorously with the flat of his chopper in the hope of making it tender. My wife, noticing a meat grinder, asked the butcher to use it. Then the problem was to keep the flies from rushing to a destiny as fatal for them as for us.

Finishing our shopping, we resumed our journey toward Lake Van. Along the way, we were fortunate to meet another traveler who let us have five gallons of gas. When we found an oasis, we camped there for the night. Raphael and I slept in the tent, and my wife and the two other children in the car.

We found no water there, so we drank the water we had brought in the canvas water bag.

The next day, our goal was Mus, which, according to the map, we could reach by a passable secondary road. Soon we were at the junction of three roads, or rather, trails. Which one should we take? We had hardly any gas left. Fortunately, fifty yards away, three men were busy loading a truckful of bricks. By paying fifty Turkish pounds for what was worth twenty, I got some gas from them and the assurance that the middle trail was the good one.

After driving twelve miles in one hour, we arrived at Gen, a new village, where only army people lived. I felt we had really jumped into the lion's mouth. We took out our map and questioned a young man, who made us understand that the Mus road no longer existed. As for gas, there was none. What with the heat, the flies, and the onlookers, I was feeling more and more irritated when another young man introduced himself pleasantly in French. A student at the Jesuits' school in Istanbul,

To reach the site where Noah's Ark rested, Navarra and his son had to climb over the main glacier at 4,000 meters. It is riddled with deep crevices as shown in this photo.

Fernand Navarra poses inside the outer extremities of the crevasse which leads directly to the Ark.

In the left photo, Raphael edges his way over to the entrance of the crevasse leading to the Ark. In the right photo, Navarra descends vertically into the crevasse where the Ark lies about 40 feet below. When Navarra got near the bottom he realized there was not enough daylight left in the day to attempt a safe recovery of wood from the Ark because he feared blocks of ice might chip off and trap him.

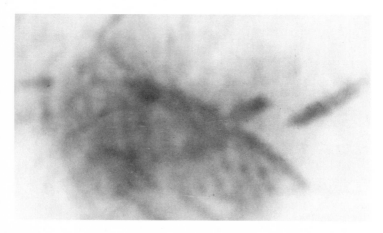

When Navarra neared the bottom of the crevasse he had barely enough light to shoot these historic photos of beams extending out of the ice and water pool on July 5, 1955. At the time these photos were taken, Navarra had not physically touched the wood nor could he get close enough that afternoon before darkness set in. In the second photo the outline resembling a fish is fragments of beams under the icy water at the bottom of the crevasse.

Following the discovery of the crevasse, a sudden snow storm hit forcing Navarra and his son to seek refuge for the night inside an igloo-like cave that had been formed by a huge boulder melting its impression into the glacial ice pack. What was thought to be a minor snowstorm turned out to be an all night blizzard which laid thirteen inches of snow on the recovery site. Navarra edged his way over to the entrance of the crevasse after the storm to determine if a descent was possible.

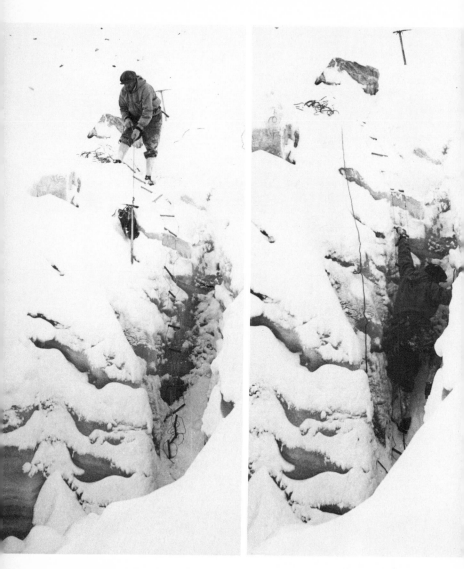

Following the blizzard, Navarra, with his enthusiasm slightly dampened, lowers his equipment into the snow-covered crevasse leading to the Ark. Then Navarra eases his way down the rope ladder into the crevasse being much more careful than the day before because of the slippery snow.

Raphael Navarra pulls the five-foot beam out of the crevasse. This beam was chopped from a much longer beam that was still wedged in the ice pack below. The crescent-shaped right side is where it was disconnected from the subterranean beam.

On July 6, 1955, Fernand Navarra posed atop the crevasse where he recovered a piece of wood believed to be from Noah's Ark. This moment was the apex of his three expeditions to Mt. Ararat to recover wood from the Ark.

he had arrived in Gen the day before to spend his vacation with his family. Could he do anything for us? Where did we want to go?

I repeated the story I had told the consul in Alep: I was an archaeologist, and I intended to do some research work; but I did not know the way, and I had no gasoline.

The young man advised me to ask either the police, or the army, or a German company that was laying a railway line in the area. I chose the third solution, and the student took us to the work site.

The executive engineer was a man in his late forties. He looked rather harsh, but proved to be quite pleasant. It was delightfully cool in his bungalow. He offered us coffee and explained the situation in a mixture of French, German, and Turkish. I understood that he would give us some gas, but he confirmed that the road to Mus no longer existed. There was only a mule trail, which even his jeep could not negotiate. There was no venturing my car on it. To reach Lake Van, the best was still to go back to Elazig and follow the main road.

I was not happy with this new itinerary. It crossed Erzerum, an important military center, where it would be difficult not to be noticed. Our chances to reach Mount Ararat were getting thinner, but there was no other way.

I filled the tank and thanked the engineer and the student, and started again. That day we drove almost 450 miles and climbed over four mountain passes, one of which was 8,850 feet high. We stopped at eleven that night. We were too tired to set up the tent, so Raphael and I slept in the open.

The sun awakened us very early in the morning, July 3. Twenty minutes later, we could already feel the heat. I checked our position; it was only forty miles to Erzerum. In a few hours, we would have to face the authorities. To be prepared, I shaved closely and put on a new shirt and well-pressed trousers. Then, just in case things went wrong, we set up an alternative project.

On our passport, we had an Iranian visa according to which we were supposed to pass through Erzerum. If our initial plan failed, we would start back toward Ankara. Raphael and I would then buy horses and try to get to Mount Ararat through secondary roads. It was a fragile plan, but the idea that we had an alternative solution built up our courage.

When we went by Askale, which had been a village in 1952 and was now a military center, I bought caps to complete our attire. It is not the cowl that makes the monk, but it helps.

Twenty miles before Erzerum, a military roadblock stopped us. I got out, and a sentinel handed me a text printed in English on a celluloid-covered cardboard. I cannot read English, but my son Fernand understands some. I gave him the cardboard and handed over our passports to the sentinel. He told us to wait and sent a soldier for an interpreter.

I had a feeling that everything was over, and soon we would have to go back. Fernand reassured me somewhat. He had not been able to understand all the English text, but had seen the words "pleasant journey." Since it was terribly hot, I took the cardboard from him and used it to fan myself. In doing so, I discovered on the reverse side a text in French:

"Stop here. Forbidden zone. Please wait a moment, for your own safety. An officer will accompany you across the zone. After having checked your identity papers, we wish you a pleasant journey."

Five minutes later, the announced officer arrived in a jeep driven by a chauffeur. Elegant and courteous, he took our passports.

He greatly admired our car. However, noticing that we did not have much room, he proposed that Raphael and Jose go with him in the jeep. They accepted, and we relaxed and left for Erzerum.

We had eaten nothing since the previous evening, and I made the officer understand that we were hungry. As soon as we had arrived in Erzerum, he took us to the town's best restaurant. When my wife went to the restroom, she saw another customer spitting in the basin. He then washed his feet in it, then his hands, and lastly his face. But it would have taken more than that to stop our appetites, and we did justice to the chicken pilau, the grapes, and the snowy sherbets we were served.

After the meal, we went to the police station, with which I was well acquainted, since I had been there in 1952 and 1953. The first time, I had arrived with the necessary permit. The second time, I had obtained it after an hour's discussion; how would things go now?

The elegant officer who had accompanied us told me to wait. Once again the specter of failure loomed. After ten endless minutes, the officer came back again accompanied by a policeman who, very politely, returned out passports, noted the car number, and wished us a pleasant journey. Saved again!

I had trouble hiding my relief, but succeeded, and even managed to be a good actor. I asked the officer to accompany us out of the town, on a road I knew as well as he, or better. Driving along together, the children still in his jeep, we passed the walls of Erzerum and crossed the fortifications and camps. Twenty-five miles down the road, at Hasankale, the officer gave us our passports and took leave of us, wishing us a pleasant journey.

The road to Mount Ararat opened up before us, free! Now, I

decided, we would go to Karakose, fifty miles from Mount Ararat. There, my wife would stay in a hotel with Fernand and Jose, while Raphael and I attempted the ascent.

At 9:00 A.M., twenty miles before we reached Karakose, we saw Mount Ararat in the distance, bathed in sunlight. Though this sight was not as new to me as to my wife and children, nevertheless, I had the same feeling of discovery. When one sees Mount Ararat, it always seems to be the first time. One of the two summits seems to be there only to make the other stand out. The harmony of the whole scene, the glitter of the snowy summit which seems, as writer Arthur Koestler describes it, to tower above the earth without a base—everything contributes to making this double mountain a unique one. Supposing there were men on earth to whom the name of Ararat meant nothing, surely even they would sense the aura that surrounds it, a kind of mystic halo, undefinable, attractive, and awesome at the same time.

At eleven in the morning, we arrived at the Transit Hotel in Karakose. The owner did not recognize me, though I remembered him. He gave us a room, in which we put all of our luggage except the mountain-climbing equipment.

At the hotel, a police officer merely registered our passports, but did not ask us for customs forms. We had a light lunch, then we tried to have a nap. But I could not sleep. The goal was so close that I lay there impatient to be up and going. At 2:00 P.M., we left the hotel, and an hour and a half later arrived in Bayazid. We took the road leading to the Russian border. In front of the *karakel* (police station), a policeman watched us go by without a gesture to stop us. Because of our caps, did he mistake us for Turks?

By 4:30 P.M., we had climbed to 7,850 feet altitude, and here we decided to separate. This was not without tears. Suddenly, I realized the madness of my undertaking. I had brought those I cherished most to this desert. Now I was forsaking some of them—my wife, Fernand, and Jose were returning to Karakose —and exposing the other, Raphael, to the dangers of the mountain. Was this egotism on my part? I wondered. I thought of the possible serious consequences, but could not relent. Even if such a thing had occurred to me, my wife's confidence would have made me brush it off. As we parted she only said, "I am sure that you will succeed, but be careful."

We kissed, took a few snapshots, and shot some movie footage. Then Raphael and I began our ascent.

iii

We hiked on the western front of the volcano, straight toward the summit. Along the gentle slope, the sun had burned the grass. For an hour we climbed steadily, till the heat obliged us to halt. Raphael, who had not cried when we parted, now began to sob.

"I did not want to cry in front of *them*, so they would not feel bad—" he explained.

Climbing to 9,350 feet, we came to the top of a spur, and in the hollow I saw two army tents. I took a picture, then turned away to avoid them. When the night came suddenly, at about seven, we had reached 9,800 feet. We kept on climbing, taking advantage of the cool of evening. We stopped at ten for the night, having reached an altitude of 11,500 feet.

Protected from the wind behind a spur, I lighted my alcohol stove and made tea. I had to be sparing of water, the scarcity of which is the number one problem on Ararat. The mountain is porous—not a spring, not a creek. Everything seeps in.

Once the tent was set up, Raphael, wrapped in his sleeping bag, went to sleep at once. But I could not close my eyes, fascinated as I was by the clearness of the night.

Worlds without number twinkled in the sky. Never, even in an airplane, had I felt so far from the earth, so close to the stars. Never had I better grasped the truth of the Bible verse, "The heavens declare the glory of God." In this immense silence, I could hear only my heartbeat and Raphael's quiet breathing.

The luminous night gave way, all of a sudden, to a magic sunrise. The first glow, lighting the icy heights of Great Ararat, turned them from white to pink, with glints of pearl and opal. Then, in turn, the graceful pyramid of Little Ararat was transformed. The shadows in the lower reaches retreated before the light, and the sun finally shone on the endless plain stretching at our feet.

Raphael woke up. We had a little more tea, folded the tent, and set forth again at 4:00 A.M. A light breeze from the west made it easier for us to start up the slope, now steeper than before. To avoid rockslides, we had to watch every step. When we had crossed a three-mile long plateau, we were thirsty again. I assured Raphael that Lake Kop was not far, but it was seven o'clock before we got there.

Lake Kop, a limpid pool surrounded by volcanic chaos, lies in a circular depression apparently an old crater. It measures about 100 yards in diameter. The water, blue and clear, tasted delicious. Its temperature was between 50° to 60° Fahrenheit.

We ate some cheese and loukoum, a Turkish sweetmeat, and drank lake water. At eight o'clock we started again. The climb was getting dangerous. Big blocks of iridescent lava rolled off when we set foot on them. Raphael had trouble following me. To make it easier for him, I would go up alone twenty yards above him, sit down, and then drop a light steel line ladder twenty yards long. Raphael would then take hold, climb up, and join me. Twenty yards higher, we would start again. When we both had tired, we stopped and took pictures.

Higher up, we had to leave that ladder, which caught in the rocks, and use a rope. Thanks to these aids, by three in the afternoon we had reached the everlasting snowfields 13,750 feet high.

Thus far I had not found the glacier which was my main landmark. When I oriented myself, I realized it was behind me. We had climbed too high. After roping ourselves together for safety, we lowered ourselves fifty yards. The wind had started blowing. It took us half an hour to arrive shivering at the edge of the glacier, which was about 300 yards wide.

The wind had stopped, but a fine snow fell. We crossed the glacier without too much trouble, for there were few crevasses, and I recognized the spot where a secondary glacier took shape, the spot where, two years before— But it did not seem that two years had gone by since my discovery. It seemed only the day before, and that I would experience the same frightful fainting spell.

Raphael's voice pulled me out of my dangerous daydream!

"Have you found the place, papa?"

"I think so."

"What about having a sleep? I'm tired."

I was tired, too. We climbed back up twenty-five yards to the north and set up the tent on hard snow.

It was 4:30 in the afternoon. While Raphael slept, I could feel the anguish which had seized me two years before. Was I going to fail so close to the goal? Perhaps I was just a few steps from the Ark, and there I was, motionless, as if paralyzed by fear. Fear of what? I felt an indefinable apprehension, a feeling of being seized at the throat by an unearthly hand.

I shook myself and suddenly remembered that in case of emergency I had brought cocaine. I took a little bit for the first and last time in my life. All at once I felt lucid, sure of myself, filled with energy—artificial energy, but as useful as the real thing. I let Raphael sleep and left the tent to reconnoiter.

Climbing up a moraine which hung a hundred yards above our camping site, I saw, on my left, a sea of clouds. Eventually it dissolved, revealing a mass of ice, the one I had discovered in 1952. The landscape had changed, for at least one third of the ice had thawed. But this was the spot.

When the mist disappeared, I recognized a wide basin on the other side of the icy mass. In this crater, the glacier's branch ended. The branch, frequently called a stagnant glacier, had receded at least one hundred yards, barely flowing into the area where the remains of the ark rested. The valley bottom was still covered with mist, and I could not distinguish a thing.

How could it be reached? Only by crawling down the crevassed moraine, as full of holes as a sponge. The stagnant icy mass was caught between two steep rock walls three or four hundred yards high. Opposite, the glacier's branch formed a smooth wall of ice fifty yards high. Between the branch and the mountain of ice was a funneled hollow covered with mist. Since the glacier had receded, there could be a lake there, where the wood from the Ark would be out of the ice.

After I had studied the problem from all angles, I concluded that the only solution would be to climb up this mountain of crevassed ice and inch down the other side of it to the bottom of the basin.

I returned to camp at six in the evening, halfway contented. Raphael, rested, had firmed up the tent by shoveling snow along the sides. We ate two pounds of crackers, then drank tea with concentrated milk added. On my alcohol stove, it took me two hours to prepare this meal. At that altitude, the pressure is too low for a gas or alcohol stove to give good heat. But since Mount Ararat is like no other mountain, the next day, at the same altitude, my gas stove worked perfectly well!

At 8:00 P.M., we went to bed half-dressed and wrapped up in our sleeping bags. In the insulated tent, it must have been about fifty degrees. To make sure that our shoes would not freeze, we put them under our pillows.

I slept that night as little as the night before. I was a little worried about Raphael, who had not yet turned twelve. I decided that in any case, whether or not I found the Ark, I would not take my son to the top of Mount Ararat.

Around midnight, the wind arose, hissing. Then a storm broke, with such frightening rumbles that Raphael woke up. "It is only a storm," I told him to reassure him, and perhaps to reassure myself. The gusts of wind were growing stronger, and the rumbles seemed to come from under our mattresses, as if the mountain were breaking up.

Suddenly, the tent fell on us. The peg which held the stake had given way. At the same time, I felt a severe blow on my knee. A loose block of lava had just hit me through the canvas of the tent.

I thought our last minute had come, but I tried not to show fear. Fortunately, Raphael's thoughts roamed far away. At the peak of the uproar, he spoke:

"You know, papa, you won't have to buy me a new bicycle. [I had promised him one.] When we get back to Bordeaux, mine will still be big enough, and then I can lend it to Jose, because his will be too small. Have you noticed how much Jose has grown since we left? Instead of buying me a bicycle, you could just buy a fountain pen for each of us."

His innocent chatter reassured me and made me hope that we would come out alive from this awful place. And the storm did die down soon. I looked at my watch; the squall had lasted hardly ten minutes. But we could still hear underground rumblings, as if the mountain had opened up inside. I lifted the part of the tent that had fallen down, propping it up with a pickaxe, and we started to doze again.

In a half-sleep, I dreamed that the snow was pink. I was watching a beautiful avalanche from a distance and asking my wife to give me the camera. But my wife was not listening, and when at last I got hold of the camera, the avalanche had stopped. I put down the camera, and the avalanche started again. Again I looked for the camera and did not find it. At last I fell asleep for good.

Raphael woke me up. "Good morning, papa. It is light, and I feel fine. Let's go look for the Ark, quick. I dreamed about it, but I can't remember my dream. Too bad, isn't it?" He added, "We should try to finish today."

"Don't be too sure of that," I said.

"I wish it were already tomorrow today."

I, too, wished it were the next day. We had our breakfast, then left the tent. All around us the ice was lined with cracks and covered with bumps which looked like molehills, from which sulfur fumes escaped. The area was strewn with blocks of lava which had fallen from the upper slopes. The block that had hit my knee must have weighed eighty pounds. Fortunately, the canvas tent had broken its fall.

In high spirits, we left the camp, hoping to make our great discovery.

iv

On July 5 at 7:30 A.M., we stood at the bottom of the mountain of ice which separated us from the site where the Ark rested. The summit of Mount Ararat shone brilliantly, but waves of fog ran along the bottom of the corridor, giving the site a sinister look. The mountain of ice which from the top of the moraine had not seemed so formidable, now loomed sixty yards above us. Though imposing, it was dangerously fragile with its crevasses and ice-bridges.

We had to climb that mass, heavy as we were with our other ladder, ropes, pickaxes, hatchet, wide-blade knives, crampons, cameras.

We attached our crampons, roped ourselves together, and began to climb. I stopped at times to film this awesome, fairy-like scene. In some places, the ice was a light blue; in others, it resembled transparent lace.

The sound of a shot, followed by a shower of stones, brought us to a halt. Had the guards whose tents we had seen pursued us? Was it an attack by the Kurds? Surely not. Kurds or Turkish guards would have been blocked by the storm. Was it a sudden storm? On Mount Ararat, two storms might break out at the same time, one on the right and the other on the left, while the weather remained calm in the center. We had climbed about halfway when we stopped and scanned the horizon, attempting to recognize some human shape among the blocks of lava.

Suddenly a muffled rumble made us turn our heads. A short distance away, a huge boulder rolled down the icy slope, leaping over crevasses, and smashing into other rocks.

That was the "shot" we had heard. A lava block had burst open with the frost.

"Take a movie, it's beautiful," Raphael urged.

I aimed the camera and filmed the rolling rock. But in my excitement I lost my balance and grabbed a piece of ice with my free hand. It broke and fell on my head, without doing much damage.

Raphael started to laugh, and his reaction reassured me. He really was not easily frightened. I got up and we kept going, but our troubles had not ended. While I was taking a movie of him, Raphael slipped and fell over the edge, still grasping his pickaxe and camera. I propped myself and tightened the rope between us with all my strength.

After a moment of frightening silence, I heard Raphael's voice from below: "The Rolex is not hurt, papa. I slipped, but I didn't do it on purpose."

That I could believe! I leaned to look down: my son had fallen about fifteen yards, stopping one yard from a crevasse. I took a deep breath, pulled on the rope, and heaved him back up.

A few minutes later, it was my turn. I wanted to show Raphael the "right way" to walk in order not to slip, and I fell too, with the Paillard camera. I fell rather hard, but I was lucky to get wedged between two blocks of ice. Raphael laughed a lot. So did I, so he wouldn't worry. But my knee that had been hit during the night was very sore. Besides, although the Paillard was in one piece, I had lost the Contaflex camera when its strap broke.

"It must have fallen lower. There is a crevasse," Raphael told me.

We looked over the edge of the crevasse and saw the camera lying at the bottom, seven or eight yards down.

I tried to fish it out with a pickaxe attached as a hook to the end of a rope. No luck. Then I decided to go down, first securing the ladder to a block of lava set deeply in the ice. An hour later, I had the camera back.

This rescue was about finished when a gust of icy snow fell on us. We took shelter behind a wall of ice. It was rather precarious; the temperature had suddenly dropped twenty degrees—to zero—and we were frozen. Raphael was wrapped so completely that I could see only a red nose and big eyes shining with pleasure.

"This is a *real* mountain," he said.

I thought it was about time he realized this.

When we set forth again after the storm, we still had to cross a maze, bordered with deep crevasses. Two hours later, we had climbed the last thirty yards, reaching the top at noon.

The first problem was solved. Now for the second one. The other side ended in a sheer wall, and we could not see what lay at its foot. If I walked too close to the edge, I feared the ice would break under my feet. How could we have a look into this hollow without falling into it?

Raphael found the solution. "Take good hold of me with the rope. I'll get close to the edge and try to see what's at the bottom."

I hesitated a moment, then agreed. I braced myself carefully and propped my back against the rock. He leaned over.

"A little bit more," he called. "More—a bit more—"

I played out a bit more rope.

"There, I can see now. Yes, the boat is there, papa. I can see it distinctly."

I almost fainted with joy, but this was no time to let Raphael go! I gave him the camera, and he took the scene in movies.

Still the problem was to reach the basin bottom. We had to lower ourselves down a bank about as high as the one we had just climbed. How? The closer we came to the goal, the more inaccessible it looked.

To try to relieve the pessimism I felt, I took a picture of Raphael sitting on a block of ice. While I loaded the camera, he walked away, the rope still around him, then called, "Come and see! There is a very deep crevasse, and you can see daylight at the bottom!"

I walked over, not expecting much. Indeed there was a deep, narrow crevasse, with light at the bottom, which was five or six yards wider than the space between the steep walls. Yes, this looked like the way down.

I uncoiled the ladder and tried it for strength. A few minutes later, I was at the bottom of the crevasse, frozen to my bones because of the humidity. A streamlet of water was running.

The light Raphael had noticed came from a corridor leading into the crevasse which was wide enough for four men of my size. It opened onto a kind of gently sloping terrace, where I got a glimpse of dark, tangled forms. Those could only be the remains of the structure I had observed from the ridge of the moraine two years before, and had so often seen in my mind's eye. I promised myself to find them again, and here they were!

I heard a bellowing noise, which at first I thought was another storm. But it was only Raphael's voice echoing in the corridor. I hurried back up and told him about my find. He was pleased, but not surprised. Nothing surprised him!

But he wanted our expedition to finish. He kept saying, "I wish it were already tomorrow, today."

I laughed. We took from our sacks tools to cut wood from the Ark. Just then, the snow started falling heavily. Fortunately, a few steps away, there was a little hollow where we took refuge. It was a real ice cave, almost square, five yards deep and two yards high—a perfect shelter for a few minutes.

We stayed there thirteen hours.

v

An hour passed, and still the snow fell thickly. To go out was impossible. As the cold grew more intense, I decided to make a small fire with "canned heat." To get one tablet to burn, I had to strike eight matches, for oxygen was scarce. Finally, I succeeded in lighting a small flame on a shovel. It warmed us up a little, but half our supply of the fuel was used. Fearing we might have to stay there longer than we had planned, I put aside the rest of the tablets.

Later on we had a meal, such as it was, with tubes of concentrated milk, to which Raphael added malt and sugared almonds.

We were really imprisoned. We could not keep on with the search, nor could we return to camp. At three in the afternoon, the sky was almost as dark as night. We could only hope that the whimsical temper of Mount Ararat would change, and the weather would clear up soon.

After emptying his knapsack, Raphael sat on it to avoid direct contact with the ice. Our eyes were getting accustomed to the near obscurity, and we examined our abode more closely. It was hollowed out like the inside of an igloo, and we noticed droplets of water running along the walls. This was comforting, as it showed us the temperature was above freezing.

Better still, I discovered that the floor of our refuge was not ice, as we had thought, but an enormous rock. It had probably fallen from the upper ridges, and had progressively sunk into the ice, leaving a hollow space, while above, the ice had formed a ceiling. Having a rock under our feet gave us a feeling of relative security which helped our morale.

Still we sat enclosed in a refrigerator, and I began to think about spending the night there. Even if the snow had stopped falling and the weather had cleared, we could not have returned to camp in less than two hours. The snow, hiding the crevasses, would have made them into death traps. And if miraculously we succeeded in reaching camp, would we have the strength to return the next day and search for the Ark? Now we were only fifty yards away. Prudence and determination told us to wait.

At six in the evening, the curtain of snow lightened, but night had come for good. Until then, we had not had time to get weary. We told each other stories, and Raphael talked a lot. Finally he got sleepy. I crouched on the rock, which seemed slightly warmer for our presence there. I had Raphael slide into the knapsack, then took him on my lap and hugged him in my arms until 11:00 P.M. I often looked at my faithful watch, which, like me, was on its third trip up the face of Ararat.

My principal concern was not to get frozen. I had heard about the sense of well-being one feels when freezing. I felt comfortable, and that worried me; wasn't this the first symptom

In 1955 when Navarra made his historic climb of Mt. Ararat he had to pass through soldiers composing a restricted military zone around the mountain which had been established to keep civilian traffic away from the Turkish-Russian border. The photo shows a typical day with soldiers doing their maneuvers while a storm is brewing over the summit of Mount Ararat.

The photo at right shows colorful young shepherd girls posing for a picture with the lower slopes of Mt. Ararat in the background. Nomadic shepherds are the only people permitted into the restricted area around Ararat without a special government permit.

The Kurds, although shepherds by occupation, are sometimes known to be hostile to outsiders and on account of them some expeditions to Mount Ararat have had to be cancelled. This was a contributing factor in the cancellation of the 1970 SEARCH Foundation expedition according to Turkish officials. Lake du Kop is one of the few lakes on Mount Ararat and the photo shows it as it appeared in 1955 when Navarra used the site as his base camp. Mount Ararat, being a volcanic mountain composed of porous rocks, has very few surface water sources because it all flows underground.

Fernand Navarra rests inside the glacierial cavity atop the crevasse leading to the ark on the night before the blizzard which nearly aborted their recovery attempts the next day. The bottom photo shows Raphael posing with the beam of the ark at a lower elevation prior to chopping it into smaller pieces for smuggling it past the soldiers. The photo gives a good size comparison of the beam in relationship to 11 year old Raphael.

Navarra in 1969 leads members of the SEARCH Foundation Expedition up Mt. Ararat to the site where he discovered the ark in 1955. In the picture they are traveling across treacherous glacial crevasses at an elevation of 4,200 meters enroute to the ark.

Navarra leads the SEARCH team to a crevasse within the glacial ice pack above the ark. Unfortunately due to heavy winter snowfalls and meager melting activity during 1969 the ark was inaccessible through the crevasse.

The SEARCH team decides to bore through the glacial ice pack with a hand drill in hopes of hitting pieces of wood with the bit. With extension poles it was possible to bore 35 feet into the ice pack.

The SEARCH boring efforts through the ice pack were unsuccessful because the bit frequently hit rocks and became permanently damaged. Two SEARCH team members survey the bit damage after a boring attempt.

Navarra with his knife attached to one of the boring poles probes a milk-white lake emanating from under the glacial ice pack. His poking and digging efforts around the edges of the lake produced small pieces of wood. The 1969 SEARCH expedition was considered successful because the team retrieved about a half dozen pieces of wood from around the lake pond. The illustration shows how Navarra descended into the crevasse in 1955 to recover wood from the Ark.

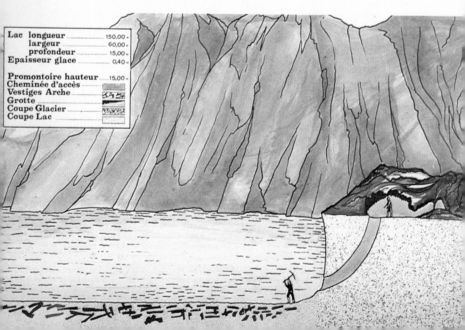

Lac longueur	150,00
largeur	60,00
profondeur	15,00
Epaisseur glace	0,40
Promontoire hauteur	15,00
Cheminée d'accès	
Vestiges Arche	
Grotte	
Coupe Glacier	
Coupe Lac	

of the freezing process? All of a sudden, I heard myself scream, "Rub my arm! I'm freezing!"

Waking up with a start, Raphael murmured, "I am cold, too."

He grasped my arm and made it turn like a windmill's sail. The pain reassured me. I was only stiff. But we had had such a close call that we broke out into a sweat in spite of the temperature.

Until morning, we exercised every half hour. At dawn, the cold grew more intense. I burned our last tablets of alcohol to warm us up and to prevent the cameras from freezing. But fire or not, drops of water no longer ran on the ice wall.

About 5:00 A.M., Raphael went out, took a few steps in the snow, and threw some snowballs. "Come out—it's warm." His voice sounded cheerful.

I joined him. The snow lay soft and white under the clear sky. We lost no time in gathering our equipment, attaching crampons, and heading toward the crevasse, in foot-deep snow.

vi

Once on the edge of the crevasse, I lowered the equipment on a rope. Then I secured the ladder and climbed down myself, assuring Raphael I would not be long.

Passing through the corridor, I found the sloping terrace and started clearing off the snow, to uncover the dark strips I had seen the day before.

Soon the strips appeared, but— This was the worst disappointment of my life. These shapes were not wood, but frozen moraine dust! It was easy to be fooled; from a distance, the mass looked like a ship's carcass. I cleared off the snow along another fifty yards. Everywhere it was the same.

At that moment Raphael's voice, distorted by the echo, came to me.

"Well, papa, have you cut off a piece of wood?"

"No, it isn't wood, it's only moraine dust."

"Have you tried to dig in?"

In my dismay, I had not thought of it! Attacking the ice shell with my pickaxe, I could feel something hard. When I had dug a hole one and one half feet square by eight inches deep, I broke through a vaulted ceiling, and cleared off as much icy dust as possible.

There, immersed in water, I saw a black piece of wood!

My throat felt tight. I felt like crying and kneeling there to thank God. After the cruelest disappointment, the greatest joy! I checked my tears of happiness to shout to Raphael, "I've found wood!"

"Hurry up and come back—I'm cold," he answered.

I tried to pull out the whole beam, but couldn't. It must have been very long, and perhaps still attached to other parts of the ship's framework. I could only cut along the grain until I split off a piece about five feet long. Obviously, it had been hand-hewn. The wood, once out of the water, proved surprisingly heavy. Its density was remarkable after its long stay in the water, and the fibers had not distended as much as one might expect.

I took snapshots and movies, then carried my wooden prize to the foot of the ladder. I attached it to the rope and left it there, for I wanted to give Raphael the joy of hauling it up himself. At last I climbed up the ladder.

Back on the edge of the crevasse, I took movies of Raphael hoisting up this ancient piece of wreckage.

It was 7:00 A.M., July 6, 1955.

vii

Our happiness, the snow blanketing everything, the fog rising around us—these made us feel as if we floated on a cloud, above the earth, apart from the rest of mankind.

As if to celebrate our victory, the sun came out and cleared the summit of Mount Ararat. While we carefully let ourselves down the treacherous slope, I was thinking about the extraordinary part Raphael had had in our adventure. He had first glimpsed the wreck; he had found the crevasse with light at the bottom, which had enabled me to reach the basin terrace; finally, he had suggested digging when I was about to give up. A child eleven years old!

I am not superstitious, but I remember that an old Armenian storyteller once told me, "To reach the Ark you must be as innocent as a child."

At 9:00 A.M., we trudged into the camp. Snow covered our tent, but we had no trouble clearing it off. We ate a few crackers and drank some coffee. Before we left, we had to find a way to carry the wood. The weight of it across my knapsack was liable to make me lose my balance, as I had discovered on our way back to camp. I decided to cut the beam in three pieces and distribute them among our sacks. Raphael took charge of it while I filmed him. I regretted having to cut up such a venerable relic, but felt better about it later on when I split it up in still smaller pieces to submit to various experts.

To make room for the wood, we emptied our sacks of everything we wouldn't need on the way back, and broke camp. An hour and one half later, we were drinking eagerly from the clear water of Lake Kop. Our thirst quenched and our flasks filled, we left by the same route we had arrived.

But we were terribly tired. It took us two hours to walk two and one half miles across a plain we had scarcely noticed on our way up. The sacks grew frightfully heavy. In spite of frequent stops, Raphael was exhausted.

I had counted on the expedition lasting five or six days. It had not lasted four, but now we were paying for over-exerting ourselves. Fearing that Raphael might not hold up to the end, I changed our route. Better meet soldiers than risk complete exhaustion. Instead of keeping on toward the west, we took the southern slope, which would lead us more quickly to Bayazid.

Half an hour later, Raphael dropped to the ground and said, "I'm thirsty, and I can't go any farther. Give me a drink."

We had not a drop of water left.

"Wait for me a moment," I said. "I'll go back up."

We had passed a patch of snow, well sheltered from the sun. It took me an hour to find it. The snow was black and almost rubbery. I sucked some, but it did not quench my thirst. I tried to fill the flasks, but the snow would not melt, and I came back with only a few drops of gray, lukewarm water.

Raphael was making sparks with two flintstones. He told me he was not thirsty anymore. Unfortunately, a quarter of an hour later, he changed his mind and the flasks gave him rather poor refreshment.

We dragged ourselves along toward the plain of Bayazid. It seemed close, but new hills seemed to arise between us and our destination. Finally we passed the last one and sank exhausted to the ground.

Almost at the same time, four gun barrels appeared, two before us and two at our sides. Behind each gun, of course, was a soldier, two of them corporals. I felt like greeting them with thanks, but refrained. Fortunately, we carried our passports, and I gave them to one of the corporals. Then I made them understand that we were terribly thirsty. The corporal told us to follow him. One soldier took Raphael's sack and another took mine, then gave up when he found it too heavy.

After a quarter hour of dragging along, we arrived at the old building they used as headquarters. One of the soldiers showed us a spring surrounded by stones almost covered with frogs. Raphael rushed over, dipped his head in, and drank in long gulps. Never mind the frogs. When I, too, had slaked my thirst, we returned to headquarters.

The corporal had emptied our sacks to make sure we carried no arms. I worried about the wood, the movies, and the snapshots.

They took no notice of the wood. They probably thought I had taken it to build a fire. But they seemed dangerously curious about the cameras. They passed them from one to another, with lots of discussion, and I expected no good from the debate. Finally, one of the soldiers, who was from Istanbul and knew a few words of French, gave me a little speech, a part of which I understood.

First, he said, the use of cameras was strictly forbidden in the military zone. Second, his colleagues and he would like their picture taken with Mount Ararat in the background. Third, if I was willing to take their pictures and send them the snapshots, they would omit mentioning in their report to the headquarters in Bayazid that I carried several cameras.

I could only accept such a generous offer. I took many pictures of them, and we left for Bayazid accompanied by two soldiers. One of them was the pleasant fellow who had spoken for them all.

Between Ararat's foot and Bayazid lies a plain of salty marshes. These are covered until mid-July with thick grass, which makes excellent fodder. Here we met a tractor pulling a trailer used for the transportation of the hay-gatherers. To our relief, they stopped and made room for us. Night was coming, too, and our companions explained that snakes infested the plain, and travel in the dark was not wise.

At eight, we arrived in Bayazid. The office at headquarters had closed, so our escorts took us to the governor's house. This charming man spoke a little French. He had lived there for six months and found his job terribly boring. Our coming made an unexpected diversion for him. The soldiers gave him our passports, and he sent for the chief of police.

While we waited, he had us sit down and asked us where we came from. "We have had a beautiful climb up Mount Ararat," I told him, quite honestly.

"Have you an authorization?"

I told him we had not. He looked surprised.

I explained that since I was passionately fond of mountain climbing, I had not been able to resist the pleasure of climbing up such a beautiful peak with my young son. This mountain irresistibly fascinated the philosopher and poet in me.

"You appeal to me very much," the governor smiled. "I like France very much. As for Mount Ararat, permits are very difficult to get. Theoretically, one must go through Ankara. But since you are here, I will take it upon myself to give it to you. I will also give you men and mules tomorrow to help you reach the top."

He had misunderstood, thinking I wanted to go up, not that we were coming back.

To have planned for a year to find some way to enter the military zone, to have succeeded only with much risk and effort, and then to be offered a way to transgress the law by the very man in charge of enforcing it—that was humorous! I was almost crying. In order not to discourteously refuse the tardy offer, I asked Raphael, "Shall we leave again tomorrow, to go to the top?"

He probably thought that I was going mad, and he sobbed, "I am tired. I want to see Mummy."

I then explained to the governor, with apologies, that I could not accept his kind offer. "If you don't mind, it will be for another time."

Fortunately, he did not insist. Meanwhile, the chief of police had arrived. He had even telephoned Karakose to make sure my family was there, as I had informed him. I asked him if I might call, too, to ask my wife to come and get us with the car. He assented, and five minutes later I was talking with my wife.

When I took leave of the governor, he made me promise to write to him, then left us with his secretary, who was as pleasant as he. This good man offered us a meal in the only restaurant in Bayazid, and that evening, we were served mutton and fruit. Then we went out on the road to watch for the car.

One hour later, I kissed my wife and Fernand. Jose had a fever and had stayed in Karakose under the care of an army doctor. At last we left, and arrived in Karakose at midnight. Jose, attacked by fever and bedbugs, greeted us joyfully. His doctor, who knew I was returning from Mount Ararat, asked, "Look for Noah's Ark?"

I merely smiled, and he did not insist on an answer.

The next day we left, and on July 11, at noon, the ancient wood specimen crossed the Turkish border without incident. Movies and snapshots came through the same way.

After a few days' rest in Lebanon, I made a kind of pilgrimage to Mount Hermon. There I found the memory of my friend Alim and the conversation which had given birth eighteen years before to the adventure now just concluded.

We passed through Egypt, where I showed the wood to an expert at the Cairo Museum. Though I told him nothing about where the wood came from, he estimated it to be 4,000 to 6,000 years old.

*   *   *   *   *

On August 1, we were back in Bordeaux. In the evening, I was counting the days we had been away, when my children saw me give a start. From Bordeaux to Bordeaux, our journey had lasted forty days—like the Deluge.

Upon my return, I was invited to relate my adventures and discovery on Mount Ararat in various countries, and I accepted the invitations. Several groups offered to help me complete the exploration once I had explained my plans.

I proposed that we organize an expedition with enough men, money, and equipment to uncover the greatest possible quantity of wood from its shell of ice and rocks, and see how the artifact was constructed. An exchange of letters followed; then the matter was apparently forgotten.

In March, 1962, a group of American evangelicals invited me to take part in their congress in the United States. They had read my book, *J'ai Trouvé L'Arche*, published in France, and wished to climb Mount Ararat in July. They requested my collaboration. I was unable to leave then, but I offered to be their technical adviser, and served in that capacity until 1968. But Crawford, an alpinist from Colorado, visited me each year to report their lack of success.

People in various places made me offers, but when I met Ralph Crawford in 1962, a close friendship developed. I promised him that if ever I climbed Ararat again, it would be with his team.

In August, 1968, I was free. Four of us secured a seven-day permit and climbed Ararat with a Turkish student. We climbed the northern face and found the site again, covered with deep snow. Then I injured my foot and could not walk. Soon afterward, the seven-day permit expired, and the police came to the camp to escort us back to the plain. However, we had achieved one thing: I had recognized the place.

This was Bud Crawford's sixth expedition. He had seen the site before from a distance, but had never thought of exploring it. Based on the findings of this expedition, the SEARCH Foundation was created, and plans were laid for the next expedition in the summer of 1969.

CHAPTER 5

The 1969 Expedition—A Diary Account

Departure from Paris (ORLY), July 7, 1969

Ross Arnold, an attorney from Atlanta, Georgia, and Harry (Bud) Crawford accompany me. We stop over in Belgrade, where Ross wants to visit a friend. We continue to Sofia, Bulgaria, where we spend the night and arrive in Ankara the evening of July 9.

Ankara, July 10

We visit our friend Doctor Rollas, who helps us secure permits for Ararat.

We apply at General Atalay's at 3:00 P.M. The reception is most cordial; the general is a friend of the doctor's. Authorization is promised, as well as the help of the army.

Bud Crawford contacts U.S. Army officials to see whether planes and helicopters might be available.

Ankara, July 11

During the day, we pay a second visit to General Atalay's and learn that certain details are missing that are necessary to complete the permit. He invites us for tea that evening. That afternoon, we are at Dr. Rollas' and find that everything is fine. He invites us for dinner. Then we go to the U.S. Embassy. They tell us politely that we can expect no help from them, neither planes nor helicopters. At five o'clock, the general's aide-de-camp fetches us from the hotel in the general's car. His wife, mother, and daughter receive us cordially. The general has asked to be excused, for he had to leave for Istanbul suddenly.

At eight o'clock, Dr. Rollas sends his chauffeured car to our hotel for us. His wife and daughter welcome us, and the family dinner is most pleasant. Dr. Rollas says he thinks the general may be able to obtain assistance from the Turkish Army.

Ankara, July 12

Dr. Rollas tells us the general has not been able to get the permit. We shall have it, but who knows when? It must come through the Internal Affairs Office. What a letdown! How much time are we going to lose? Coco (my son) and Ralph Lenton, from the Arctic Institute of North America, are to arrive on Monday evening, and are we ever blue!

Ankara, July 13

We pass a miserable day. We swim in the hotel's swimming pool, tour Ankara with Ross and Bud, seeing Ataturk Mausoleum.

Ankara, July 14

At ten o'clock, Dr. Rollas telephones us at the hotel. We must go to the general and get the permits. The doctor and the general, in a joint action, secured them yesterday. That afternoon, after much discussion, we leave the office with the signed permit. We cable Washington, asking the other two members, Hugo Neuberg and Fred Lee, to join us. Tonight Coco and Ralph Lenton will be with us. We must thank the doctor. At last we are satisfied. At Ankara Airport we pick up Coco, but do not see Ralph. Returning, we find him at the hotel.

Ankara, July 15

Still no planes or helicopters are available. We will have to travel by minibus. The equipment and the other two members are to arrive on Thursday evening. Mr. Ross would like to visit Cappadocia, so tomorrow we'll drive there and test the minibus at the same time.

Ankara–Urgup–Ankara, July 16

We depart at 6:00 A.M. and arrive at Urgup by eleven. We visit Urgup, Goreme, and Ushkicheir. It is a beautiful day's travel for Ross, Bud, Coco, and me.

We return to Ankara by ten in the evening.

Ankara, July 17

Nothing in particular today. In the evening, Fred and Hugo arrive at the airport with our equipment. It will have to go through customs tomorrow. Reunion at the hotel; we agree that we must leave as soon as possible. Mr. Arnold will leave tomorrow for the United States.

Ankara, July 18

The customs authorities will not clear the equipment. In the morning, Coco and I accompany Mr. Arnold to the airport. To get through customs, Bud will ask Dr. Rollas' help. At the end of the day, we are asked to leave a deposit, which we will see about tomorrow. Our team seems like a splendid, cooperative group. I think we shall get a lot of work done. Coco agrees with me that Hugo Neuberg is the "boy scout" type. Bud Crawford has a friend who is a U.S. Army colonel, and we are all invited to the officers' mess for lunch. We enjoy an excellent meal.

Ankara–Corum, July 19

We have succeeded in getting our equipment through customs. At 6:30 P.M., we leave in our minibus. Dr. Rollas has come to say good-bye. Two and a half hours later, we arrive at Corum, where we shall sleep. According to my itinerary, we should have slept at Samsum. We are 120 miles behind schedule.

Corum–Samsum–Ordu, July 20

We leave Corum at six in the morning and have breakfast in Samsum. Hugo leaves to look up a friend stationed in a U.S. Army camp in Samsum. He comes back two hours later to tell us his friend has invited us for lunch. This means a *six-hour* halt. I'm beginning to wonder whether this is an expedition or a holiday.

It is late, and we find a good hotel on the Black Sea shore. We stop for the night. I expected to reach Trebizonde! Two hundred and fifty miles behind schedule, and Hugo wanted us to set up a tent and do our cooking to save money!

Ordu–Trebizonde–Erzerum, July 21

Hugo has filmed a few scenes, but he is slowing us down. He stops our bus a little too frequently to take pictures. I get provoked with him and tell him things cannot go on this way. Another problem is that we have no designated head for the expedition. I propose Bud Crawford, and everybody approves.

My role will be that of an adviser, and all agree. By evening we are in Erzerum. We have made up 190 miles.

Erzerum–Dogu-Bayazid, July 22

It is 7:00 A.M. We were to leave at five, and the minibus driver is not here yet. He shows up at nine. His excuse is that he had understood we were to stay five days in Erzerum. He's a sharp one.

We're off. At 2:00 P.M., we reach Agri (Karakose), where we visit the governor, a charming man, and he speaks French. I think he is a little suspicious about our intentions. Why do we intend to spend three months exploring Ararat? He asks many questions about the Ark, religion, and our intentions if our expedition succeeds.

We learn that he has read my book, and he would be glad to have Ararat become an important tourist center. He countersigns our permit, and we leave with a letter of recommendation for the vice prefect in Dogu-Bayazid.

Late that afternoon, we arrive in Dogu-Bayazid, where we visit the doctor's nephew, the commanding officer who is to help us. We find he was transferred to another area the week before. No help from the army. Although it is late, the vice prefect will see us. The chief of police is with him. The vice prefect can speak French, so he, Coco, and I agree on a plan. Tomorrow morning at eleven o'clock in Ortulu, a hamlet at the foot of the Ararat, we are to meet four guides, thirteen horses and donkeys, and seven or eight drivers—a good expedition. According to my schedule, we are only one day late. After a full day, poorly started but well ended, we check into Hotel Kent, which we find excellent in every respect.

Dogu-Bayazid (Altitude 10,500 feet), July 23

We are up at 7:00 A.M. After a shower, a shave, a good breakfast, and a few last-minute purchases, we take leave of the vice prefect. At ten, we leave in our minibus. Twenty-two miles of plain separate us from the foot of Mount Ararat, yet from Dogu you'd think you could reach out and touch it. It's beautiful! It's 11:00 A.M., Ortulu. All is ready—guides, horses, donkeys, donkey drivers. At 1:00 P.M., the caravan is ready to leave.

We have eleven pack donkeys, four guides, and nine drivers. We each ride a horse. The horses are good enough, but the harnesses are poor. I have only one stirrup. When I ask for the second one, I am told that this horse is used to one only, and that he would refuse to go if another is put on.

Hugo, who had never ridden before, is the first to fall. Bud is the second, because of a broken harness strap, which might have happened to any of us. The ascent goes well. We ride by a camp of shepherds who are friendly. We halt at 5:30 P.M. and settle for the night. We sleep well at this altitude.

July 24 (Altitude 10,500 feet–12,300 feet)

Reveille is at 3:30 A.M. It is dawn already. We eat a light snack and load the equipment on the pack animals again. I shave, and the shepherds cannot believe their eyes. They think I am a barber, and they all want their beards trimmed. They are pretty clever. I say, "Wait until tomorrow."

After climbing one hundred yards, the expected happens: my harness breaks, and now it is my turn. I must pull the horse instead of riding it. We arrive at Kop by 11:00 A.M. We argue with the drivers, who do not want to go around the lake, for the

75

shore is rather steep. The guides agree with us, and after an hour's discussion, the drivers give in. When they shout, you would think they are going to cut each other's throats. In fact, they are more like quarreling children.

At 12:30, we reach the other side of the lake, where we set up camp. The shepherds kill a young goat and cook it. At 3:30 P.M., the drivers leave us with their horses and say good-bye. We have two guides and three porters, one driver having become a porter.

At 4:00 P.M. we begin, with the porters' help, to carry up the two cases of equipment, weighing 100 pounds each, as close as possible to our goal, which is almost 14,000 feet high. Kop is 12,300 feet up, and we take the cases up to 12,800 feet. This is the spot where we shall settle our home camp tomorrow. We go to bed at 7:00 P.M.

July 25 (Altitude 12,800 feet–13,500 feet)

Reveille at 4:00 A.M. A bit cold, but beautiful weather. We carry our equipment up to 12,800 feet, after prospecting for a spot to set up our camp as close as possible to the site of the Ark. In the evening, 1,500 pounds of equipment arrive at the 12,800 feet camp, and 250 pounds at 13,500 feet on the way to the site. We all feel rather tired and sleep well.

July 26 (Altitude 12,800 feet–14,000 feet)

About six o'clock, everyone gets up. Out of five, only Bud is feeling fine. Coco has hurt his knee, so he will watch over the camp. At 7:30, Bud, Fred, Ralph, Hugo, and I leave for the site, looking for the best way to reach it. At 9:30, Bud and I are on the spot. It is a beautiful place. It seems that, although I left in 1968, it was only yesterday.

Following their historic find and recovery of wood from the Ark both Raphael and Fernand Navarra rested and had a meal of dried fruit with coffee before making their descent from Mt. Ararat.

The awkward beam presented much difficulty when it came time to carry it off the mountain. It being extremely difficult to handle could easily create a tragic accident for the climbers if they did not find a suitable way to carry the beam. Finally Navarra licked the problem by strapping it onto his back and carrying it like a knapsack.

When Fernand and Raphael reached a lower elevation, they realized that trying to carry such a huge beam past Turkish soldiers would attract suspicion and even arrest due to the fact they did not have a permit to be on Mt. Ararat. Both Fernand and Raphael pose with the beam for one last time, before it is chopped into smaller pieces. Note the shape and length of the beam.

Navarra chops the beam into four pieces that will fit into their knap-sacks. They hoped that if the soldiers checked them, they would believe this historic artifact was merely firewood which was not used by the two campers.

At the base of Mt. Ararat, the Navarras did encounter Turkish soldiers who were rather disturbed because these two campers had been on the mountain. But after taking several photographs of the soldiers with Raphael posing with some of them, all suspicions were dropped and the troops even provided transportation back to the nearest city in their tractor wagon.

The top photo shows the positions of the three pieces if the beam were refitted. The bottom photo is a close-up of a piece of wood which is in a near carbon state (also pictured on the extreme left in the top photo). Tests by leading universities in Europe have dated the wood at approximately 5000 years.

The top photo is of another portion of the wood which according to Navarra has been hand squared while the bottom photo shows a piece of wood which has been hand hewn.

Navarra holds a piece of wood, greatly deteriorated, which has been both hand hewn and squared. The bottom photo shows a piece of wood recovered by Navarra during the 1969 SEARCH Foundation Expedition. It is encased in a special container to prevent further deterioration.

The space between the northern and southern moraines is 140 yards long and 70 wide. The icy snow has gone down two or three yards. I recognize certain spots, in spite of changes in the glacier and new-fallen debris, on the northern and southern moraines. In 1968, the edge of the glacier was a huge mass of ice. Now, thanks to the thaw, it is like a large clump of lace. In the lower area, we discover a crevasse twenty yards long, four yards wide and five to six yards deep. We go down with our ladders and we see, looking through the cracks, that it resembles a huge Swiss cheese, very dangerous to explore but fairy-like and entrancing. The snow is soft; we sink in up to our waists. We take a few movies and some snapshots, and we climb back up to the hard ice shell.

On the side of the northern moraine, the ice has thawed from the sun's reflection on the rocks. A nine-yard-deep hollow has formed. We lower ourselves into it easily thanks to our crampons. Three-quarters of the way along the bottom we discover part of a lake, halfway frozen. A surface of ten by eight yards is in the open, and the thawing shell forms a cave twenty-five yards deep, ten yards wide, and five yards high. The water from the thawing ice overflows the lake, which spills between the rocky wall and the ice- and rock-encrusted glacier's outer shell. Thus the water tunnels underground. At times, the lake's water rises as much as one and one half feet, increasing the overflow. We discover the underground stream, thanks to its rumbling sound. At 2:00 P.M., we go back. Although tired, we are pleased with today's progress.

July 27

Up at four o'clock. Bud will accompany Ralph as far as Kop Lake. He is returning to the United States. Fred will stay at the

12,800 feet camp. Hugo, Coco, and I leave for the site. Apparently, the day will be clear. We intend to take our drilling equipment to the spot and leave it there. Coco carries the fifty-pound drill, Hugo has the ten-pound detector, and I have thirty pounds of extension tubing for the drill.

At ten o'clock, everything is in place. After a short rest, we begin our first hole. Everything is going well. After ten minutes' drilling, we are three yards deep. Without much trouble, we reach six yards; then the bit apparently hits a rock, and we stop drilling. We start again four yards away, and have to stop twenty minutes later. On the third hole, we reach eight yards and damage the bit, but it is not serious. On the fourth and fifth tries, same results.

At 12:30, we are tired and stop drilling. There are not enough of us for this job. The altitude and scarcity of oxygen get us. Drilling may be a good idea, but it is a tiring one. It gives us a good chance to film action, and these movies add zest to the expedition. Hugo tries out his water-depth detector. On the film, it will look very scientific, which is well and good, but it doesn't give us tangible results.

At 2:00 P.M., we are back at the 12,800 feet camp. Bud has cooked a meal. After we eat, two shepherds, armed with pitchforks and big sticks, visit us. They worry me. We invite them to eat. Hugo does all the talking, since he wants to learn Turkish. Personally, I am writing and thinking about my badly shaven Americans, my two armed Turks, our camp, and the campfire surrounded with stones Coco has assembled.

The scene reminds me of a gold rush. When I think about it, we are in the same situation, looking for the vein. I don't know why, but I am convinced we will succeed. In 1955, I mused, I had found the lower end of the glacier in a lake where a construction emerged, which looked to me like the Ark. This spot is noted in the accounts of all those who have seen it. On July 6, 1955, at the beginning of the summer, I found this lake frozen, but by the end of the month it must have thawed. Nineteen fifty-five was the geodesic year known to all glacier specialists, when glaciers were at their greatest point of thaw. With these beautiful thoughts and expectations, I go to bed.

July 28

We are up at four o'clock, and leave at six, Bud, Coco, Hugo, and I. Fred will watch over the camp. We try another slightly steeper way, crossing three névé fields. We had put on our crampons from the start. We arrive at seven o'clock feeling more and more fit. Our intention is to drill until twelve o'clock or exhaustion. The weather is beautiful, the sun warm with a cool wind blowing. I hope it lasts. While Bud, Coco, and Hugo get ready to drill, I go visit the cave and the lake. I note that during the afternoon, the inside has thawed quite a lot. The lake is pouring out more water than two days ago. This is good for us. Tomorrow, Fred will begin serious filming.

It is 8:30 A.M. The bit is four yards down and cannot go deeper. We start another hole. An hour later, we are eight yards down and hit more rock. Another spot, one hour later, nine yards down—rock again. This time we damage the bit. On the fourth try, same result six yards down. It is 12:30 P.M. We are very tired and abandon the job. We get back to the camp at 1:30 P.M., rather disappointed. In the afternoon, the weather deteriorates. Big clouds blow up, and it is quite cold. During the night, a hailstorm hits which does not last long. We have a good rest.

July 29

We arise at four o'clock. The weather is good, though it froze during the night. Everyone is ready at 4:30. Bud did not sleep well—he had fleas. He had let one of the guides use his sleeping bag, and that is what he gets for it. He will stay at the camp.

During the night, we all suffered from fatigue, lack of oxygen, and the storm. That is Ararat. Fairly fit, Fred is going to film. He has prepared a scenario. I am confident in his ability; we should have a good documentary.

At six o'clock, we leave. We were to take movies, but at 10:30 we are out of film so we explore the lake and the crevasses. The weather is neither good nor bad. There are rock slides around us. Now it is hot, now it is cold. We drill two holes three and nine yards deep, and cannot go deeper. By 1:00 P.M., we are back at the camp, very tired. Hugo feels slightly sick. Bud is well rested. Coco takes care of the cooking. At seven, we go to bed.

July 30

Rest today, for we are all in bad shape. I get up at seven and make breakfast. All night long, we have heard avalanches. The weather is threatening.

We study the digging possibilities. Bud and Hugo propose to open a hole wide enough to go down with ladders. Bud wants to go to Dogu-Bayazid to buy two more spades and picks. That is not necessary. If we adopt this digging idea, one spade will be enough for the four of us, and I am sure it will not be used half of the time because of lack of oxygen. Everyone agrees.

I note this morning that the time goes by fast, and that we are getting weaker every day. I shave daily, and this morning, Bud and Fred have shaven, too. A shepherd and his young son visit us, and we offer them tea and biscuits. They have a young hare they want to give us to roast, but we decline.

Hugo wants to drill again. I suggest that he drill along the moraine directly in the side of the outer shell, thus gaining seven yards on its thickness. However, avalanches are to be expected, and he will have to be careful. Bud and I will explore the thawed part of the lake. We'll use the drill extensions, to which we will tie our hunting knives or our ice picks. Thus we should be able to feel out the bottom of the lake. At the same time, even if we find no remains of the Ark, we can at least take movies to show its exact location.

It is noon. I go back into the tent and sew up my leaky sleeping bag. I am fidgety; my thoughts roam. What wouldn't I give to succeed? It is really disappointing. You leave in high spirits, you are full of dreams, you have made your plans. It is easy, success is near at hand. Living at 13,000 feet is like a game. Working here is child's play. There is camping, outdoor living, feeding on canned goods. An air mattress is fun, sleeping bags are good—it's real living. Let's get on with the discovery quickly. What are we doing here in camp? We're losing time.

We had left home full of joy and confidence. Then in Ankara, we had delays getting our permits to explore. We had valuable support, but for four days our spirits alternately soared upward, then fell. Then the U.S. team arrived. We had difficulties clearing the equipment through customs. At last, here we are on the mountain.

After 900 miles in a minibus, jostled with equipment and luggage, we arrived thinner and tired. Now we are here, at an altitude of 12,800 and 14,000 feet, camping, eating, sleeping on mattresses that lose air in the middle of the night while the sleeping bags lose their feathers, which then tickle our noses. In the middle of the night, we gasp for oxygen. Sometimes I wonder what I am doing here again—I was so well off at home. At my age, why didn't I stay on the plain, serving only as a counselor for the expedition? What pushed me into coming? Pride? If that is the reason, I am paying for it. In 1952, when I returned from my first expedition, people said, "Navarra believes in fairy tales. He wants to bring back Noah's Ark. He is as crazy as those who think of going to the moon." Yet, this very month, men have gone to the moon and come back.

While repairing my sleeping bag, I prick my finger, and the pain clears my thoughts. I say to myself that, pride or not, suffering or not, we must succeed, we must exhaust all possibilities. This Mount Ararat enterprise is like any calling. The time is limited, days go by, you think things go wrong. In spite of everything, you gird yourself, you try harder, try not to be discouraged, stay optimistic, hope to finish in time. I call this philosophy "the rainbow." Why should Ararat be an exception? In this life, contentment is found in struggle and effort, so let's be patient and keep on.

With these new resolutions, I feel better. I come out of the tent and find the weather has deteriorated. Coco is cooking, the soup smells good, and I begin to sing at the top of my voice. Coco answers back, and our chorus surprises our friends. Our gaiety brings back a smile to all those thin faces.

The menu: soup, meat balls with onion, dried vegetables, stewed fruit—a real banquet. It is one o'clock, and the meal will be ready around three. In the meantime, I read. At three o'clock we eat, and the food tastes good. Congratulations to our chef, in spite of a few traces of moraine dust we crunch between our teeth. At seven, everyone goes to bed, and until midnight we listen to the storm, the hail, and the avalanches.

July 31

I get up at four o'clock and make tea. The water takes long to boil. It has been freezing again, but the weather is beautiful, with scarcely a cloud over Ararat, which looks like a snowy bonnet from Brittany or Normandy.

I bring the tea, but the men don't feel like getting up. In spite of the sunshine, a north wind has us shivering. Hugo is still sick and will not come with us. I leave with Bud, Fred, and Coco. Fred is in top shape, and he takes all the movies he can.

We arrive on the site at seven. We use our new method, exploring the lake with the drill extensions after fixing a hunting knife on one end. On the other rod, we fix a pickaxe. The lake is thirty feet deep. We take turns stabbing, hoping to hit a piece of wood, and we scrape around the edges. An hour and a half later we have found nothing. We shift to a new location, exploring the big crevasse below the lake. We put a ladder down and climb inside. It is thawing everywhere, and there is a strange sensation of warmth. We sink in up to our waists. We stab with our harpoon as far as five yards down. A one-ton block of ice breaks loose and nearly hits us. After an hour's investigation, with the ice running like rain water and the place now dangerous, we climb back up and rest.

We talk over the situation. We can explore three spots: east, north, and west. The western point is the highest part of the site where the remains are. The eastern part has the big crevasse. The northern part of the site has the big moraine with the partly thawed lake and the overflow pouring down the mountainside.

We shall go back to the lake and explore the overflow stream and its rocky bed.

Coco and Fred are filming on the dome. Bud and I go back to the lake. We stab, we scrape. The water gets milky. Ice blocks float up to the surface. It is hard work. On one side, the moraine crumbles away, causing small avalanches. On the other side, the ice melts under our feet. Now we are at the overflow. With my pickaxe, I widen the opening and pull out stones. By my side, Bud scrapes the walls.

Suddenly—I don't know whether Bud loosened it by stirring the bottom or whether I pulled it out from the overflow opening—but we both glimpse a black rectangular object in the moraine mud. It floats, then sinks again, and leaves us dumbfounded.

The wished-for "rainbow" has come. It is a marvelous moment. I seem to be floating on a cloud. I have a confirmation of what I never doubted, proof that what I found in 1955 was not a mere accident. Bud holds this piece of evidence in his hands. It really is wood, the same kind that I brought back in 1955. It is 11:15. We shout with joy. We call Coco and Fred, and we are all happy. Bud is crying. It is his seventh expedition. At last, after all our ordeals, we can locate what we call "Noah's Ark."

Let us not get involved in a debate on what this wood means. One fact is certain: there is wood on this part of the Ararat, and it has been there for a long time. Now we are sure we can devise a plan to dig out all that can be found, and we must do it. We take a careful hold of our souvenir, and we keep on searching, assisted this time by Fred and Coco. We are excited, but tired. Satisfied, we put away our tools and hike back to the camp at

12,800 feet. It is two o'clock. We have our meal and a needed rest. At three o'clock we hold a meeting and decide:

1. Bud Crawford will go down to Bayazid and cable "Father" Crawford and our friend Ross Arnold to tell them the good news, and tell the guides and porters to get their horses and donkeys ready for us. We will go down the mountain Sunday at 11:00 A.M. At this point, Bud leaves, planning to spend the night at a shepherds' camp.

2. We will make filmed sequences of the discovery. We will also take measurements to locate the remains accurately. We shall also keep on exploring to the limit of our strength. At 7:00 P.M. it is dark already, and we go to bed. We sleep restlessly, but have beautiful dreams.

August 1

This morning we stay in bed late. I get up at six. The weather is perfect. I leave with Coco, Fred, and Hugo, who now feels better. At eight o'clock, we are on the site. Hugo tries to drill, but without result. The big crevasse on the dome is thawing and enlarging rapidly. It is too dangerous to explore. Upstream, we find another crevasse that has opened. It is very deep, and it is too dangerous to be explored today. We'll try tomorrow.

We return to the lake and explore again. We are hindered by the falling rocks. We scrape relentlessly. Hugo and I go into the cave from which the lake comes out. No luck there either; the vein has disappeared. We begin to feel weariness, and go back to camp exhausted. Coco has hurt himself again, this time his left arm. It is not serious, but he has a bruise and a few cuts. We eat good hot soup and take a nap. Then we sum up our results: we have made one find. Tomorrow Fred, Hugo, Coco, and I shall explore again. Hugo wants to drill one last time on the side of the dome.

August 2

We are up at four. At six, Fred, Hugo, and I are ready to leave for the site. Coco isn't feeling well, so he will stay at the camp. The weather is not very good. During the night, we heard a storm. Certain parts of the mountain are covered with snow again.

We return to the site. Fred films large panoramic views. When the sun finally breaks through, a big ship of ice seems to take shape on the site. It is very strange.

The big crevasse has grown still wider. It almost thaws before your eyes. Hugo keeps on with his scheme—he wants to drill into the side of the dome. We need Coco and Bud, for Fred is filming. With only two of us, we decide not to go down the big crevasse, which is dangerous for two people only. We agree to go back to the pond. The outflow has lowered one and one half feet. There is scarcely half a foot of water in the overflow channel. After we have scraped and stabbed for half an hour, we start to dismantle the vault-shaped roof of the channel. With our axes, we dislodge large blocks, weighing 200 to 400 pounds each, which drop into the lake. We open up about four feet of the roof as far down as the first curve in the stream. Hugo labors like a miner with his spade, pick, and hands.

Suddenly, from a mixture of rock and mud, Hugo brings out another piece of wood eight inches long. He gives a shout of jubilee and starts an avalanche! Fred comes to take movies. We are delighted and excited. We keep on digging and pulling out rocks. It is hard work, but thrilling, and life is wonderful again.

The weather is hot and close, and we are perspiring, but we can't stop digging. A quarter of an hour later, Hugo finds a piece of wood sixteen inches long, and his yell starts another rock slide. It's wonderful. We find a few more small pieces. We want to follow the stream down to a sharper curve. This time we dig in the ice, trying to break up the blocks, but they are too heavy. We are exhausted. We rest for ten minutes, then twenty, then thirty. But the weariness remains, and finally prevails over our enthusiasm.

Because of the altitude and gradually diminishing strength, we decide to put an end to the search. We take part of the equipment down with us. I leave with Fred, who films a few last scenes of this beautiful mountain which, in spite of our ordeals, has given us so much contentment.

Before we reach the camp, we come to a wide, rather steep névé field sloping down one hundred yards. We slide down this simply by sitting down and letting gravity take over. Previously we slid down only half or two thirds of this snowfield this way. This time, to end the search, we slide down all of it. What fun! Fortunately this is the last time, for our trousers have no more mileage in them. Fifty yards lower, we arrive at the camp. Coco is overjoyed to hear of our new discovery.

We eat soup and rest. At 4:30 Bud comes back from Bayazid. When he sees all this newfound wood, he sheds another tear. Good old Bud. He really deserves this happy ending.

Tonight, we go to sleep contented, for we have found even more than we expected. Our patience has been rewarded.

August 3

We are up at five. Bud and Hugo climb up to the site to explore a little and bring back equipment. Coco, now fit again, will bring down the drilling equipment in four trips. Four porters are to arrive at eleven, and we shall move and set up camp at Kop Lake, where the donkeys and horses can come.

We prepare the luggage. At noon, the porters have not arrived yet. At 3:30, Bud decides to carry the small tent to the lake and sleep there with Hugo. Coco and Fred will take part of the equipment there, then come back to the 12,800 feet camp for the night.

While waiting for them, I prepare our last meal: soup, steaks—which I fry in margarine—peas, and stewed fruit. The soup has been cooking for half an hour, and I taste it fairly often, without thinking. My mind is elsewhere, as if in a daze, when rolling rocks startle me out of my dream. Here comes the young shepherd, the one who offered us a rabbit a few days before. I had given him a knapsack with a shopping list of things to get in Bayazid. I did not expect to see him again. What a nice boy! From this sack I take out five nice tomatoes, six pimientos, three cucumbers, three onions, one loaf of bread, and cheese. I thank him heartily. If his face were clean, I would kiss him.

After a while, he makes me understand that he wants to leave, so I pay him for his errands. To show me how thankful he is, he sings a tune for three minutes. When he has finished, just to be polite, he bows to me and disappears among the rocks. His departure makes me sad. After a good meal, very gay, we go to bed at seven.

Around eleven at night, shouts awaken us. There come our porters. They claim they are on time. They say they understood the appointed time is 10:00 P.M. Perhaps we shall never know the truth. They tell us that horses, donkeys, and animal drivers are waiting for us 200 yards lower down. Three of them stay with us in the tent, and the last one goes to tell the others that we shall start at dawn. We go back to bed.

August 4

Reveille at 3:00 A.M. I make tea. At four, we have five porters. Two of them will make the trip twice. Coco, Fred, and I, with the five porters, will carry everything down without going through Kop, following a shorter route. As we descend, we find a chaos of unstable rocks weighing at least half a ton each. The grade is very steep. It is beautiful, but dangerous. Half an hour later, down on the plain, we send Bud two horses and two drivers. At nine, our whole group is together. We have seven horses and six donkeys. I am offered a horse, which I turn down. I'd rather walk and arrive safely in Bayazid. I don't trust the harness. Coco and I walk in front with a guide. We have had so much practice walking that we often have to wait for the caravan, since we are too far in front. I even believe that the guides have trouble following us. We stop at two shepherds' camps. Bud knows the leaders, and they offer us *aynan* and yogurt. They are truly friendly.

The farther down we go, the hotter it gets. By early afternoon, we arrive at the bottom of the first foothills in Ortulu, where clouds of mosquitoes greet us. We shall keep the marks for the next ten days. Ortulu is eighteen miles from Dogu-Bayazid. In between lies a plain of salty marshes yielding top-quality fodder for winter feeding of cattle.

The minibus and Jacob, its driver, are waiting for us. At three o'clock, the luggage is piled in. We say good-bye to the guides and porters, adding a few little gifts, and also distribute a few lumps of sugar to our brave donkeys, so strong and so valuable on their thin little legs. An hour later, we arrive at the Hotel

Kent in Bayazid. We take showers, change clothes, and my companions have a shave. At last we are presentable.

It is evening, and we find three surprises waiting for us at the hotel:

First, we meet John Libi, who is to leave tomorrow to explore Ararat. It is his fourth or fifth attempt to find the Ark. Until now, he has had no luck. Once he lost one of his men and another one was injured. On his other attempts, bad weather kept him from reaching the site. We are introduced, for we have not met before. We converse politely, but say not a word about our accomplishments or their plans.

Our second surprise was meeting Dr. Lawrence Hewitt, Dr. Clifford Burdick, and Eryl Cummings, whom I have known since 1962. They are also leaving tomorrow to explore the Ararat. Greetings, polite talk on both sides, but no mention of the results of our expedition. Also, nothing about their plans.

The third surprise, the most pleasant, is to find my good friend Colonel Sehap Atalay here. What a pleasure to get together! We embrace like sentimental old brothers-in-arms. In 1952, he was a lieutenant at the head of a company of soldiers when we climbed the summit together. I shall remember him forever as an exceptional man in every respect. I had arranged to have our climb filmed, and I had given the document to the Turkish Army. Imagine how happy we are to meet again after seventeen years.

We reminisce about our joys and pains. It seems as if we remember every detail of our trip, in spite of the years passed. Speaking French, he tells me he will guide John Libi up Ararat, but he does not say a word about the search for the Ark. I know he is familiar with the site, and know that in 1958, he brought back a fragment of wood.

I invite him for dinner, but he cannot accept, for Mr. Libi has had a table set in his honor. I do not insist.

The head waiter has carefully organized his tables. There are three rows, separated by empty rows. One table is for the John Libi team, then an empty row, and our table separated from Dr. Hewitt's team by another neutral row. Since we are in the middle, we are often addressed by one or the other team. I am almost facing Sehap, and we propose toasts to each other. The atmosphere is full of electricity all around, for each team has an air of quasi-secrecy. Still, we are all friendly.

After a good meal, contented with a day full of unexpected events and pleasant surprises, we go to bed.

Dogu-Bayazid–Erzerum, August 5

We arise well-rested. After breakfast, I see Mr. Burdick, who offers me a bucketful of freshly cooled grapes. I accept, and the whole team enjoys them. They are delicious. Burdick is a charming man. We speak in Spanish together. Later on, he wants to take a movie of me and my son, and I accept. An hour later, they leave in an army vehicle. John Libi's team had left around five in the morning.

At nine o'clock, we say good-bye to the vice prefect, Mr. B. Camit-Bayar, and to the chief of police. We have a pleasant conversation, and let them understand that we are very pleased with our achievements. The vice prefect seems happy about this. He is the one who greets all the explorers, singly or in teams. If they haven't an authorization from Ankara, he gives them a permit. He hopes that the presence of the Ark, testified to by the sacred books of the three great monotheist religions, will make of Ararat an important place of pilgrimage.

We leave Dogu-Bayazid at 10:30. Twenty-five miles away, we have a last look at Ararat. Our hearts are a bit heavy. It has brought us a lot of suffering, but we love it.

In the minibus, I get to thinking. Should one of the other groups find remains, as we have, it would be better to have our find publicized as early as possible. First, we will wait till Ross Arnold and Ralph Crawford arrive from the United States, which will not be before August 12 or 13. This means another week. I propose that tonight we telephone from Erzerum to our Turkish friend, suggesting that he ask Arnold and Crawford to speed up their journey, so that before the end of the week we can give an official statement to the press. My companions agree.

We arrive at Erzerum and go to the Haman. We call our Turkish friend, who approves of our plan. Then we call the States, and Arnold and Crawford also approve. We set an appointment in Istanbul, at the Tarabaya Hotel.

Erzerum–Ankara, August 7

We depart at seven and arrive in Ankara at two in the afternoon. We go to the Kent Hotel, take a bath, have an excellent meal, then a good night's rest.

In the evening, around seven o'clock, when I went out to buy a few things on the boulevards, I was surprised to meet Memet, a student from Aralick who accompanied us to Ararat in 1968. We exchange cordial greetings, but he seems to speak guardedly. Is he expecting another team from the U.S.? He was to come to the hotel to say hello to Bud, but did not show up.

What should we think of that? The year 1969 is a competitive year for Ararat.

Ankara–Istanbul, August 8

We leave Ankara in the morning and arrive at the Tarabaya Hotel, Istanbul, at 4:00 P.M. Istanbul is a city of 2 million inhabitants. Modern factories stretch along sixty miles of the road leading to it. Fifteen miles have been made into a motorway. The modernization accomplished in seventeen years is nearly unbelievable.

Ralph Crawford arrives with one of his friends, George Wakefield. Our Turkish friend is here, too. Ross Arnold shows up a little later, and during our meeting, we decide to call in the international news agencies the next day at 6:00 P.M. Then we have a good rest.

Istanbul, August 9

We meet to write up the official statement to be made to the press and work out the next stages of our mission. At 6:00 P.M., we are interviewed by the reporters, all of whom are most interested in our findings.

The 1970 "SEARCH" Expedition

Although Navarra's name was mentioned frequently in fund raising efforts by SEARCH Foundation of Washington, D. C., during 1969–70, he did not participate in the 1970 expedition. This was largely because Navarra believed SEARCH Foundation was inefficiently organized and unwilling to cooperate with other exploration groups interested in the quest for Noah's ark.

The 1970 expedition included several SEARCH corporate

board members, and two scientists from the University of Michigan. These scientists scaled Mt. Ararat, set up camp near the excavation site, and waited for the SEARCH team to arrive. When they did not arrive, the scientists returned to Ankara where they discovered the SEARCH team had had their climbing permits revoked.

Associated Press and government news dispatches from Ankara, dated July 12, 1970, disclosed the following reasons for the cancellations:

1) The Turkish government's unstable political situation and fear of international criticism.

2) Some Turkish newspapers claimed the U. S. Central Intelligence Agency was involved in the expedition.

3) The government feared possible foreign involvement in resurgent separatism among Kurds, who live in the vicinity of Mt. Ararat.

4) Nervousness in Moslem Turkey about the connection of the Christian church with the SEARCH Foundation.

5) A Turkish crackdown on smuggling ancient treasures out of the country into American and European museums.

6) SEARCH's lack of cooperation with other groups seeking to do further research on the same project.

7) A diplomatic incident involving one of the SEARCH team members.

In light of this Mr. Navarra has decided not to lend support to or participate in any expedition which does not serve the interest of *all* the various American and European groups, or which does not have the full approval of the Turkish government.

94

Any inquiries concerning this book should be directed to:

Fernand Navarra
84, Boulevard George V
33000-Bordeaux, France

U. S. Agent
Dave Balsiger
257 Brentwood Street
Costa Mesa, California   92627

APPENDIXES

The Deluge According to Assyro-Babylonian Tradition

The Legend of Berose

The Legend of Berose, a third-century B.C. Chaldean priest, author of a history of Chaldea and Assyria, is known to us only through excerpts given by Eusebius of Caesarea in the third century A.D. It is evidently related to the story of Genesis. However, the author insists that his sources were not biblical, but from ancient historical documents of his country.

In his account, the god Chronos appears to the tenth antediluvian king, Xisuthros (or Sisuthros), and announces that soon all men will perish in a deluge. He enjoins him to take the beginning, middle, and end of all that has been recorded before him and bury it in the City of the Sun, in Sippara, then to build a ship and take refuge there with his family and dearest friends. Xisuthros builds a ship, five stadia long and two stadia wide, fills it with food supplies, and gets aboard with his family. When he asks Chronos which harbor he should head for, the answer is, "Sail to the Gods" ("Sail to the Heavens"). The Deluge comes, engulfs the rest of mankind, then recedes. Xisuthros lets a few birds go, and they come back, having found no dry land. A few days later, he lets them go once more; they return with mud on their feet. Let loose a third time, they do not return. Xisuthros then notices that his vessel has stopped on a mountain in Armenia.

Berose adds that in his time people could still see the remains of Xisuthros' ship on the Gordyan mountains (ancient name of the region situated between Kurdistan and Lake Van; therefore, the Ararat region). The natives would scrape off the asphalt coating, to which they attributed curative or even supernatural powers.

The Gilgamesh Epic

A Chaldean version of the Deluge, more ancient than comes from Berose, was found on tablets discovered on the site of Nineveh, in the middle of the last century. These tablets, from the library of King Assurbanipal (669–626 B.C.), nearly 25,000 in all, were stored at the British Museum for many years.

In 1872, an amateur Assyriologist, George Smith, announced that he had deciphered the cuneiform writing of one of the tablets. Though incomplete, it contained a new account of the Deluge. The following year, he had the extraordinary good fortune to find another fragment in Mosul, and this enabled him to complete the first text. These documents constitute what is known as "The Gilgamesh Epic." The account of the Deluge is only a part of the whole.

Gilgamesh, the hero, is a giant, half man and half god. He cannot reconcile himself with the death of his friend Enkidu. He becomes conscious of the fact that he himself will die one day, and goes to visit his ancestor Ut-napishtim to inquire about the secret of immortality. Ut-napishtim answers that one must merit immortality. He has won his own by surviving the Deluge, of which he gives an account.

Sickened by men's wickedness, the gods have decided to destroy the earth. But the god Ea wants to save his protégé Ut-napishtim. He tells him to build a boat and take the seed of all life with him. Ut-napishtim does as he is told. He builds the ship and goes aboard with his family and animals.

The Deluge comes, which lasts for six days and six nights. The morning of the seventh day, Ut-napishtim looks at the weather. Everything is silent, and all mankind has gone back to mud. The ship has run aground on Mount Nisir. Ut-napishtim lets loose a dove, which flies away but comes back. A swallow which does the same, and finally a crow that finds corpses to feed on and fails to return. The passengers land and offer the gods a sacrifice. The gods have an argument: Enlil, their king, blames Ea for saving Ut-napishtim. Ea pleads his protégé's cause, and abates Enlil's anger so well that he grants immortality to the survivors.

THE EPIC OF ATRAHASIS

This is the third Assyro-Babylonian version of the Deluge. The Epic of Atrahasis parallels that of Gilgamesh. Atrahasis, "The Very-Wise," seems to be one with Ut-napishtim; like him, he is warned about the Deluge by Ea, who traces an outline of the boat on the ground, for his protégé has no experience in naval construction.

Such are the main Mesopotamian versions of the Deluge. Andre Parrot has compared the texts and summed up his work in his small volume *The Deluge and Noah's Ark.* The account in Genesis and the others deciphered from the cuneiform show a surprising resemblance. In both, there is divine determination to destroy mankind because of its crimes; warning given to one man, with recommendation to build a boat; boarding of the chosen one and his family; destruction of the rest of mankind; the sending of birds.

The parallel between the two traditions is evident, though there is disagreement as to which preceded the other. Parrot believes the biblical account to be the Israelite version of a Mesopotamian tradition, imported by the patriarchs who emigrated into Canaan. The description of the Ark and the idea of navigation tends to point to the Babylonians, who knew more about seafaring than the Hebrews.

Incidentally, Parrot's book reveals the greatest skepticism as to the preservation of the Ark. Though he climbed Ararat, he was not trying to prove anything as regards the discovery of the ship.

As to my own pursuit, the question of which version preceded which was of secondary importance. I needed no exact dates. If I succeeded in finding the remains of the Ark, working out the historical truth would be greatly facilitated. I simply accepted as true the biblical account; this was my "working assumption."

My research brought me many a surprise. I learned that there were not two or three, but twenty or thirty different accounts of the Deluge. Many different peoples had their own version of the catastrophe, with salvation given to a few through divine favor. Bossuet was right when he asserted that "the tradition of a universal deluge is found the world over."

The Deluge in Other Traditions

"Not only the Aryans and the Semites, but almost all the people on earth have placed a struggle against the liquid elements, represented by a major disaster, at the beginning of their history."—Renan

EUROPE

Greek and Latin mythology give us two main versions of the Deluge. Ovid writes about the first one, originally told by Apollodores of Athens. The box—more exactly, the vase—of Pandora was not enough to exterminate the human race, so Zeus decided to flood the earth. Prometheus warns his son Deucalion, King of Thessaly, and advises him to build a large chest into which he will climb with his wife, Pyrrha. The chest floats nine days and nine nights. On the tenth day, the Deluge ends, and the chest lands on Mount Parnassus; Deucalion gets out and offers a sacrifice to Zeus Phyxios, protector of Fugitives. Zeus promises to grant his first wish. Since the human race was annihilated by the Deluge, Deucalion asks Zeus to give it life again. Zeus tells Deucalion and Pyrrha to pick up stones and throw them over their shoulders. The stones that Deucalion throws become men; those that Pyrrha throws become women.

In a second version, the Greek Noah is not Deucalion, but Ogyges, founder of Thebes. Mount Parnassus sometimes gives way to Mount Othrys Geramia, in Thessaly.

The Greek story seems to be derived from the Babylonian tradition. Possibly a Hittite tradition provided a link between the two.

Welsh, Icelandic, and Lithuanian legends also tell of a deluge. In the Icelandic version, the flood is provoked by the blood running out of a giant's wound. The Lithuanian tale has the supreme god, Praamzio, angered by man's iniquity. To punish him, Praamzio frees two monsters who are in constant struggle: Water and Wind. Taking hold of the earth, the monsters shake it for twelve days and twelve nights, destroying all life with the exception of a few couples of men and animals who have taken refuge on the top of the highest mountain. From his celestial abode, Praamzio beholds the disaster while eating the sacred nuts that grow in the celestial gardens. When the water reaches the top of the mountain, he drops a nutshell. The survivors climb into it, and neither Water nor Wind can do anything against this god-given vessel. At last, Praamzio's anger dies down. He puts the two monsters back in their prison, the water ebbs, and the rescued couples re-populate the earth.

Finnish-Ougrian mythology is related to that of various people such as Siberians, Magyars, Finns, and Lapps. Their version of the Deluge story probably comes from Islam, founded on Semitic sources. However, it contains one original feature: as the animals enter the ark, Noah's wife also lets in the devil.

ASIA

An account of the Deluge appears in the Zend-Avesta, the sacred book of ancient Persia. The story appears to have been borrowed from Semitic sources, but with one peculiar detail: the refuge is not an ark or vessel, but a *vara,* an hypogeum, an underground tomb or fortress.

The reign of Yima, the first man and first king, is a Golden Age. It is interrupted by the disaster, brought about by the Demon Mahrküsha's evil spell. Ahura Mazda, the creator of the Universe, warns Yima and instructs him concerning the building of the hypogeum and the choice of the species to be put there: "You will build a *vara,* a horse's run long, as wide as it is long. There you will take every species of animals, big and small, men, dogs, birds, oxen and sheep."

Since the refuge was not to float, the material was not wood. When Yima asks, "How shall I make this *vara?*" Ahura Mazda answers, "You will knead clay with your hands and feet, as the potters do."

*   *   *   *   *

The Hindu myth does not exist in the Veda, but in the Satapatha Brahmana (sixth century B.C.). While washing himself in the river, Manou, the Hindu Noah, finds in his cupped hand a tiny fish which begs him to let it live. Manou puts the fish into a jar. The following day, the fish has become too big, and Manou must throw it into the lake. The fish continues to grow until the lake gets too small for it.

"Throw me into the sea," the fish asks, which Manou does. Grateful, the fish warns him of the imminent deluge and advises him to build a boat. Manou obeys. Once the Deluge has come, the fish pulls the ship toward a mountain in the north. After the water has receded, Manou offers a sacrifice to the gods and is granted a young woman. The human race springs from his union with this woman.

According to the Mahâbhârata, Manou, upon the fish's advice, takes seven wise men with him on the ship and seeds of all species. The fish's head is armed with a horn, to which Manou ties his boat. The fish pulls the boat to the highest peak of the Himalayas, Mount Himavat (Ship's Anchorage), which gives the peak its name. After the Deluge, thanks to ascetic practices, Manou creates all living things: gods, half-gods, men, animals, and plants.

According to the Matsyu Purâna, the gods themselves build the boat on which all animal and vegetable species take refuge. The Bhâgavata Purâna gives the same story, only the hero's name being changed: Satyavrata, an ascetic. Finally, according to the Agni Purâna, the warning fish is Vishnu himself, while in the Mahâbhârata the fish is Brahma.

The myth of the Deluge exists in Southeast Asia, but it is difficult to separate the native traditions from those of Hindu, Islamic, and Christian origins, the latter introduced by missionaries.

The case of China is peculiar. There, according to tradition, a huge flood took place in 2297 B.C. Only one Fah-Le, his wife, and three children escaped. Not the sea, but the overflowing of rivers caused the flood, and it was stopped "by the swelling of the sea." Possibly this refers to a gigantic tidal wave, which they called the Deluge. This agrees with the testimony of Georges Lanoë-Villène in his *Livre des Symboles.*

A ninth-century Arab traveler, Ibn-Wahab, a parent of the

Prophet, was granted an interview with the Emperor of China. The conversation touched on the Deluge, and the Emperor said he had heard about it, but that it was only a local phenomenon which had not reached his country.

Burma also has its diluvian legend, as do Filipinos. The latter tradition says that only a few privileged people escaped by climbing high mountains. When they believed that the punishment was sufficient, the gods permitted the water to run away through a hole in the ground.

Africa

The Egyptian deluge is not a punishment, but a blessing. We know about it thanks to an inscription on Seti the First's grave, in Thebes. Irritated by men's crimes, the god Ra destroys almost all of them. The few survivors offer him a sacrifice which appeases him. Ra promises never to destroy mankind again, and as a token of his good will, provokes a flood that will fertilize all of Egypt.

In Africa, among the Masai traditions, we find a deluge as punishment for murder. There is a saving ark and four rainbows announcing the end of the plague. This appears to be of Semitic origin.

North America

Alaskan Eskimos have a traditional account of a formidable flood with a simultaneous earthquake. The few who survived, fled in their canoes or took refuge on the highest peaks.

According to an Arctic Eskimo legend, the chosen people made a raft by fastening several canoes together; they huddled

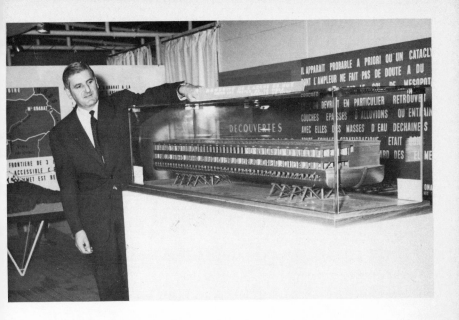

These photos depict a museum exhibit prepared by Navarra in France. In the top photo he poses by a scale model of Noah's Ark, which he designed after studying numerous historic documents. The bottom photo is a display case containing the three main pieces of the wood from the Ark.

Another display in Navarra's museum exhibit is a scale model of Mt. Ararat with details indicating where the find was actually made. The bottom topographic map indicates the geography of Mt. Ararat and in particular where they made their camp at Lac de Kop (Lake of the Summit).

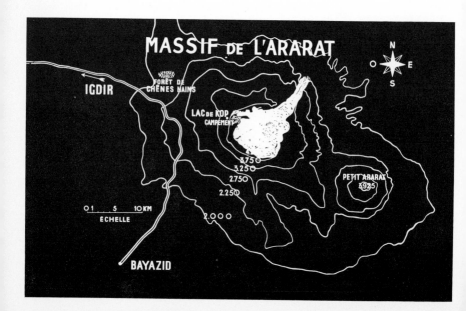

This topographical map shows the various routes taken by Navarra in his expeditions on Mt. Ararat in 1952. The first climb departed Poste Militaire D'Ahora and ended at Moraine Frontale at 7,375 feet. The second attempt departed from Campement Yusuf Tozu and ended at 13,000 feet near Glacier Inferieur. The third attempt to reach the summit departed from the southern approach and was successful with Navarra reaching the 16,934-foot summit on August 14, 1952. The fourth climb made by Navarra was in search of the Ark. It departed and ended at D'Ahora. Just above Lac De Kop on this climb Navarra sited the remains of Noah's Ark, but did not reach the actual site for recovery attempts until 1955.

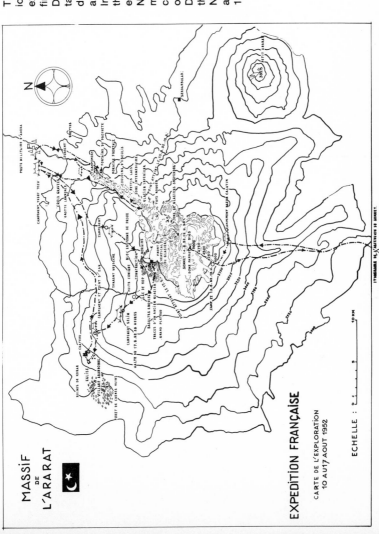

MASSIF DE L'ARARAT

EXPEDITION FRANÇAISE

CARTE DE L'EXPLORATION
10 AU 17 AOUT 1952

ECHELLE :

Some of the documents which Navarra consulted in his research on Noah's Ark and its appearance include this ancient cuneiform tablet at the British Museum in London.

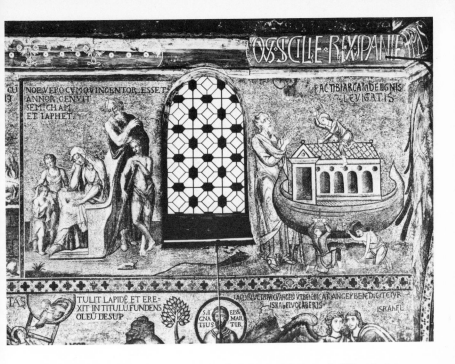

Many biblical scholars as well as artists have speculated on what Noah's Ark may have looked like. The top photo is of a mosaic on display in Israel. The bottom photo is of a painting done about the 12th century now on display at the St. Savin Church in Vienna.

A Romanesque capital at St. Lazare Church in Autun picturing the ark balanced atop Mt. Ararat. One of the oldest representations of the Ark in France, it is, according to Navarra's research, closer to the true appearance of the Ark than the typical boat-like concepts of the previous page.

Two views of a model ark which Navarra built after years of research in ancient Akkadian, Sumerian, Armenian, and Hebrew writings. The top photo is a side view showing air vents along upper and middle side. The bottom photo shows interior compartments through a cut-away.

LAMINA I.

Muestra problema:
Quercus pedunculata
Ehrh.

Sección transversal × 20

Sección tangencial × 20   Sección radial × 20

These photographs show the fiber structure of the wood recovered from Mt. Ararat by Navarra. Scientific tests (see the appendix) revealed the wood to be a type of oak about 5000 years old.

LAMINA II.

Muestra testigo:
Quercus pedunculata
Ehrh.

Sección transversal × 20

Sección tangencial × 20   Sección radial × 20

together to protect themselves from the icy wind. A sorcerer, An-odjim (Son of the Owl) throws his arrow into the sea, then his earrings, and cries out, "Enough, Wind! Abate!" The tempest then dies down, and the water retires.

In the diluvian legend shared by Algonquins, Iroquois, and Hurons, the "Great Har," Michabo, goes out hunting with the wolves he uses as dogs. The wolves dive into a lake and remain prisoners. While Michabo is looking for them, a bird comes and tells him where they are. Michabo decides to go into the lake to get the wolves out, but the water overflows and covers the whole earth. Michabo charges the raven to find a bit of clay for him, which he remodels into a new world. The raven fails. Michabo then sends an otter, which dives in, but without success. Finally Michabo asks the muskrat, which succeeds in bringing him back a bit of clay. Once the earth is remodeled, Michabo also restores the trees by shooting arrows in the dead trunks, which sprout branches. Then he punishes those who kept his wolves in the lake, and marries a muskmouse. This marriage will repopulate the world.

CENTRAL AMERICA

For the pre-Columbian Mexicans, Noah might be represented by Imos, a patriarch who built a large skiff to escape with his family from the Deluge.

For the Aztecs, a Babel-type confusion of languages follows the Deluge. The disaster wipes out mankind with the exception of one man and one woman, Coxcoxtli and Xochiquetzal, who board a boat and reach Mount Colhuacan. Saved from the flood, Coxcoxtli and Xochiquetzal have many children, but they are mute until the day when a dove, perched high in a lofty tree, bestows the gift of language on them. Unfortunately, the languages are so numerous and so different that the children cannot understand each other.

For the Luigenos in Lower California, the Deluge submerged the highest mountains except for the Bonsald heights, where the survivors had taken refuge.

SOUTH AMERICA

The Araucanians in Chile also tell of a legendary mountain refuge, but this mountain, Thegtheg, has a peculiarity: it is a floating mountain. The Araucanian deluge originates from an earthquake and a volcanic eruption. When the earth trembles, the Araucanians gather food supplies and make for the summits.

In one provincial legend from Peru, the adviser (analogous to the fish in the Hindu legend) is a llama:

"Once an Indian tried to tie up a llama in a good pasture, but the animal resisted and showed his sorrow, in his own way. 'Idiot,' his master said to him, 'Why do you complain? Why do you refuse to eat? Isn't the grass here good?' 'You fool,' the llama answered, 'you must know that I am not sad without a reason. In five days the sea will rise up and cover the whole earth.' The Indian asked if there would not be some way to escape. The llama told him to gather supplies for five days and follow him to the top of a mountain. The mountain was called Villca-Coto. The Indian obeyed. When he reached the top of the mountain with the llama, he saw that a host of birds and animals had already taken refuge there. Then the sea began to rise, covering the plains and mountains, except the Villca-Coto. Even then, it came so close that the fox's tail dipped in the water, and that is why the end is black. The sixth day, the water level lowered, and the sea returned to its normal bed. But all men lay dead except one, from whom all people on earth descended."

The "floating mountain" of the Chileans parallels the "growing mountain" of the Canari Indians in Ecuador: this mountain grows as the water rises, thus enabling two brothers to escape the disaster. Two brothers, twins Tamenduare and Arikute, are the heroes of the legend of the Tuscaroras Indians in Brazil. Tamenduare is a good husband and father, while the other fights and does evil deeds. One day Arikute comes back from a fight brandishing the arm he has torn off an enemy. He shows it to Tamenduare and challenges him, "Get out, you coward! I shall keep your wife and children, for you are not brave enough to protect them." To this Tamenduare answers, "If you are as strong as you pretend to be, why don't you bring here the whole body of your enemy?" Furious, Arikute throws the severed arm against his brother's door. Immediately the whole village is taken up to heaven, and the twins are left alone on the earth. Reconciled before the danger, the twins flee to a mountain with their wives and climb the trees. To know how high the water is, Arikute picks a fruit, gives it to his wife, and tells her, "Break it and drop a piece." From the noise the falling fruit makes, the brothers know the water is still high, and they wait. Finally, the two couples are the only survivors, and Tamenduare and Arikute give the earth their descendants, who go on fighting as the two brothers did.

Escaping by climbing trees is a theme found in several Indian versions of the myth. But sometimes the men who climbed the trees become monkeys, while those who fall into the water become fish. In other cases, the myth of the Deluge is associated with the creation of the world: the flood has transformed the earth into a vast ocean and the Demiurge recreates it.

The Carayas Indians of the Amazon also have a legend: "One day the Carayas hunted wild pigs. They forced the game out of cover and killed them. They dug into the ground and found a deer, then a tapir, then a white deer, and finally a man's foot. Frightened, they fetched a wizard, Anatina, who succeeded in unearthing the man by singing, 'I am Anatina! Bring me some tobacco!' The Carayas did not understand, and offered him flowers and fruit, which he refused, showing them a man smoking. They understood and brought him tobacco. He smoked on and on until he fell unconscious to the ground, and the Carayas took him to their village. There he woke up and began singing and dancing. The Carayas fled away, terrified. Anatina called them and told them to stop. He ran after them, taking many calabashes full of water. Since they kept on running away, the wizard broke one calabash, and immediately the water began to rise. They were still running, so he broke a second calabash, then another, and yet another, and soon the whole country was flooded except for the mountains at the mouth of the Tapirapis, where the Carayas took refuge. Then Anatina gathered all the fish and asked them to pull the men in the water. Several tried, without success. Finally the bicudo (a fish whose long mouth resembles a beak) climbed the opposite side of the mountain and took most of the Carayas from behind, throwing them into the water. Only a few Indians held onto the summit and stayed there until the end of the deluge."

Oceania

In Samoa and New Britain, a legend says that in the beginning the sea was only "a small quantity of salt water, which one man kept locked up and hidden. Others tried to take it away, but when they lifted the lid of the box, the water poured out and caused the flood."

Australian natives had several Deluge legends. One says the flood was a punishment inflicted on men for catching a sea monster. According to another, a frog swallowed all the water on the earth. The eel succeeded in making it laugh. The frog, throwing back the water, caused the disaster. In a third version, black swans are men who, at the time of the Deluge, took refuge on a mountain; they were changed into swans when the water reached their feet.

In Melanesia, the Deluge is sometimes attributed to a fish-demon's vengeance.

One fact has been noted by Alexander Haggerty Krappe in his *Universal Mythology*: "The Myth of the Deluge is known to Polynesians, under various forms which have enough originality to exclude any Biblical influence."

From this brief recital of diluvian legends, several conclusions can be drawn. First, we note the universality of the myth; many different peoples have heard about the Deluge.

Does this mean that all peoples have known a Deluge, or that some thirty disastrous floods have occurred? Or only one universal flood, of which each community has kept a memory? And has each people interpreted the flood according to their own primitive genius?

The Ark: What Was It Like?

THE DESIGN

Since I wanted to find the remains of the Ark, I had to have as accurate a picture of it as possible. So I studied the biblical text and its many commentators. In St. Lazare Church in Autun, I discovered, there is a Romanesque style capital picturing the ark balanced atop Mount Ararat. It is one of the oldest representations of the Ark in France. It is naïve, but perhaps close to the truth, for the Ark probably looked less like a boat than a house. Most likely it resembled a huge floating box (like Deucalion's "large chest") without keel, mast, sails, oars, rudder. It was not meant to navigate, only to float until the water receded.

This houseboat, its walls covered with asphalt inside and outside, had three stories, or decks. It was divided into compartments, with one window at the top.

At the beginning of the seventeenth century, Peter Jansen, a wealthy Dutch merchant, had a scale model of the Ark built, following the measurements given in Genesis. This model, 120 feet long, twenty feet wide, and twelve feet high, proved to hold one third more than vessels of current design with corresponding tonnage. This design was judged safer and called for a smaller crew.

Origen, the "father of biblical exegesis," has written a chapter on the Ark in his *Homilies on Genesis.* Origen's opinion is valuable not only because he, like St. Jerome, worked on writings now lost, but also because during his travels through Palestine, he gathered many oral traditions.

What does Origen say about the shape of the ark? "Judging from the description, I imagine that it had a rectangular bottom and that the walls converged gradually as they rose to the top, where the width was only one cubit."

Why this shape, of a house rather than a boat? Origen answers, "Given the conditions resulting from the rain and Deluge, a more appropriate shape could not have been given to the ark than this narrow summit which let the rainwater run down, like a roof, and this rectangular bottom flat on the water, keeping the ark from pitching or sinking under the action of the wind and the waves or because of the animals' restlessness."

Origen poses, and solves to his satisfaction, the question of the "product of digestion" of the animals shut up in the ark. "Tradition relates that the lowest part in the hold was set apart for necessities of that kind. The part immediately above was used for stocking food supplies."

THE DIMENSIONS

As for the dimensions, Genesis gives them specifically: 300 cubits long, 50 cubits wide and 30 cubits high. If we assume that a cubit equals 18 inches, this would mean 150 yards long, 25 wide, and 15 high.

How was Noah, even if helped by his sons, able to achieve such a construction? Some answer that it took him more than a hundred years. It seems reasonable that when the narrator writes, "Thus did Noah, according to all that God commanded him, so did he," it does not mean Noah did it alone or only with the help of his three sons. The account credits the shipbuilding to the main character just as the Bible says Solomon built the Temple in Jerusalem. We also say that Louis XIV built the Chateau de Versailles and Napoleon the Arc de Triomphe. In other words, they took the initiative in the building; quite evidently they employed many others.

Another question often asked is, "How could an ark of the given dimensions have held all the animals?"

The Dutchman Tiele figured that over 6,000 species, one couple per species, could have found room. However large this figure, it is still far from the hundreds of thousands of creature species which must have existed in Noah's time. How could the patriarch gather this fabulous flock and get it into the Ark?

Most Church Fathers have not even considered the question, for they estimated the number of animal species at a few hundred only. But Origen noticed the contradiction, and he proposed an imaginative solution. Instead of reducing the number of animals, he increased the size of the ark! "Geometricians, he says, have a way of calculating what they call 'proportional,' according to which, for volumes and surfaces, one cubit represents six cubits."

As far as we know, few have taken this novel proposal seriously.

A mid-nineteenth-century Italian Jesuit, Father Pianciani, has suggested a theological solution: "Since the Deluge was a punishment for men's sins and not for animals' sins, it was normal that all men should perish in expiation of their faults, but not all the animals who had nothing to pay for."

THE WOOD

More mysterious is the question of the material used for the building of the Ark. The wood fragment I brought back from Mount Ararat has been identified by experts as a kind of oak, but this may be only part of the framework of the ark, and not of the walls or roof. The material expressly named in Genesis is gopherwood, which a dictionary defines as "unidentified wood used for the building of the Ark."

Modern translators of the Bible, such as Canon Crompon, translate *gopher* as "resinous wood." St. Jerome translates, *"Fac tibi arcam de lignis laevigatis"* (Make yourself an ark of planed pieces of wood), while the version of the Seventy says *xula tetragona,* "of quadrangular wood." Several commentators have wondered whether the word *gopher* meant a particular kind of wood of the cedar or cypress family, or a wood worked in a special way. Others have considered *gopher* a copying mistake, or a contraction of *gophrith* which means brimstone.

Mount Ararat—"Mother of the World"

"And the ark rested in the seventh month, on the seventeenth day of the month, upon the mountains of Ararat" (Gen. 8:4). Many traditions, Jewish, Armenian, Persian, Turkish, or Tartarian, agree that the Masis area is where mankind was saved and born again. Thus, they considered Ararat the world's center, the "Mother of the world."

(True, in the Gilgamesh Epic, Ut-napishtim's boat lands on Mount Nisir; and the Moslem tradition selects Mount Djudi [or Al Djoud], situated farther south. But Mount Nisir could not be located exactly, and as for Mount Djudi, Islamic commentators have their private reasons for selecting that mountain.)

There is hardly a place near Mount Ararat whose name does not recall Noah's story. Nakhitchevan—Naxuana for Ptolemaeus—was called *Apobaterion* (landing place) in Josephus' time. Its present name means, "the place where Noah landed," and the traditional place of his grave is still shown. Erivan can be translated as "'the first appearance." Arguri (another name for

Ahora) is "the planting of vine." European and Semitic winegrowing originated, as Alexander Haggerty Krappe points out, from this area where Noah, according to the Bible, "planted a vineyard."

The Turks call the mountain Aghri-dagh (Mountain of the Ark) and the Persians call it Kok-I-Nouh (Mountain of Noah).

It is generally admitted that in the Bible the word "Ararat" means a country or region—Armenia—not a mountain. And it is true that the three other passages where it is mentioned (Isa. 31:38; II Kings 19:37; Jer. 51:27) refer to the "country of Ararat" and the "kingdoms of Ararat." But if we admit, as commentators do, that Ararat and Armenia mean the same, it appears that the "mountains of Ararat" (mentioned once only, in Genesis) would designate what we call "mount Ararat" today.

Could Noah and his family, after leaving the Ark, have descended the slope of Ararat? This is not beyond human possibilities. I have had the experience five times. Besides, it is logical that the receding water first uncovered the highest summit. Mount Ararat is not only the site where the Ark lands; it is also the place where God speaks to Noah, promising him never to curse the earth again because of man, and offering him divine blessings. In the Bible, many a solemn encounter between God and man takes place on a mountain.

Ararat has been called the "Mother of the World." This idea of center, in the case of Mount Ararat, compels recognition. Equally distant from the Black Sea, the Caspian Sea, and the northern part of the Mesopotamian plain, Mount Ararat is the central spot of the line of plateaus which extends from the Bering Strait to the Cape of Good Hope. For these reasons, it has been considered "not only as the historical center of the Armenian plateau, but also as the center of gravity of the ancient world."

Mount Ararat is a volcanic group with a double summit, Great Ararat and Little Ararat, which covers 400 square miles. In the southwest, it overlooks the plateau of Bayazid, 5,000 feet above sea-level. In the north, it borders the alluvial plain of the Aras River with an altitude of 2,950 feet.

The main characteristic of Mount Ararat is its apparent isolation, which gives it a striking appearance. In the west, it is connected to the volcanic chain of the Aghri-dagh, which itself joins the Taurus chain and the southern part of the Anti-Caucasus chain. Nevertheless, you get the impression of a soaring monolith. This is not only illusion, for although Mount Ararat, with its 16,900 feet, is not nearly so high as Himalayan and other summits, it is the first when you measure its height above the land surrounding it. It stands 14,275 feet above the plain of Etchmiadzin, while Everest, Elbruz, Chimborazo, and Mont Blanc overlook the neighboring valleys only by 9,800 feet to 13,000 feet.

From base to summit, Mount Ararat displays four color zones: a grayish zone, of mixed sand and volcanic ash; a grassy zone which turns yellow in the summer under the drying action of the sun; a black zone made of basaltic rocks; a dazzling white zone of everlasting ice and snow.

The mass is made of igneous rocks of a porphyroid type, resulting from intense volcanic activity which shaped and reshaped the northwestern part of Asia several times. Mount Ararat is a volcano, but a strange one, with no crater on top. However, there are craters on the sides, particularly on the southwestern slope of Great Ararat.

During historical times, no eruption of Mount Ararat was recorded until 1840. That year, on July 2 a little before sunset, the ground was shaken by undulating waves from the Great Ararat to the east. Fissures appeared on the sides of the mountain, and gas fumes burst out, hurling stones. The ice cap was shattered. Witnesses heard a rumble for an hour within the mountain.

The village of Ahora disappeared, also the monastery of St. Jacob which had stood for eight centuries. Of the 2,000 and some inhabitants, a hundred only survived—those outside the village itself when the quake struck.

The shock reached Erivan, Nakitchevan, Bayazid, and Makou in Iran. Over 6,000 houses were destroyed. The Aras River overflowed and flooded the plain. In the riverbed, craters opened up and water under pressure of the gas spurted up in geysers. A few days later, an avalanche of mud from the mountain slopes destroyed the areas spared by the quake. Water from rain, mountain streams, and thawing snow had almost liquefied the earth.

Traces of the disaster are still visible. In many places, the fracturing of the rocks looks quite recent. The 1840 catastrophe far exceeded the usual earthquakes which are so frequent in Armenia.

The German naturalist Moritz Wagner has proposed an explanation of the great 1840 earthquake. Those who have explored Mount Ararat have noticed how dry it is, and many have suffered for lack of water. Why should this be, since the melting snow at around 13,000 feet gives birth to innumerable streamlets? Because the streamlets disappear, absorbed in the rock and underlying ashes. Where do these streams finally end up?

After visiting Mount Ararat himself and studying this phenomenon at length, Wagner concluded that a huge underground lake must exist beneath the mountain. He further theorized that through an underground fault, the lake may have come into contact with the old heart of the volcano, and this contact would have caused the 1840 convulsion. Since the old crater had been blocked for centuries, the explosion followed the line of least resistance. The water from the lake put out the underground fire, which explains why there were none of the usual volcanic manifestations—neither lava flows nor spurts of flame.

Of course, no geological theory could convince the inhabitants of the Ararat region. The disaster simply strengthens their conviction that Mount Ararat is "evil mountain," and that a curse is connected with it. So it remained for a dozen explorers or so, from the beginning of the nineteenth century to the present, to explore fabled Mount Ararat and seek to uncover her ultimate secrets.

Documentation on the Wood Testing

National Museum of Natural History
Comparative Anatomy of Living Plants
and Fossils
61, Rue de Bufion, Paris

March 7, 1956

Dear Sir,

I am enclosing the result of my examination of the wood you gave me.

I hope this work pleases you, and I ask you to be assured of my best wishes.

Ed Boureau,
Under Director of the Museum

APPENDIX V

Mr Roger Grosjean
Attache to the National Centre of Scientific Research
43, Rue Laffitte   Paris

Examination of a Wood Sample Consisting of ....

The specimen which was given me appears to be a slice of the dimensions 4cm X 9cm X 13cm, the large surface being a cross-cut.

It is a black color and comes from a thick trunk, if one judges from the annual rings and from the angle of the ligneous sections.

Transverse Cut: The transverse plane shows wood of porous areas in the initial wood, with large expanding pores divided on two concentric circles, abruptly becoming much smaller pores in dendritic arrangements in the final wood. The annual rings have a thickness of from 2 to 4mm, which for a tree indicates active growth.

Tangential Cut: The sections of wood have a dark cellular content, but much darker than that of present oak wood. The sections are of two types: very large dense sections, and small, even sections. The tracheid fibers are covered with typical areolated markings.

Conclusions: This wood belongs unmistakably to the oak *Quercus* of the type *Leucobalanus* and very probably to *Quercus robur*.

Ed Boureau
Under Director of the Museum

Minister of Agriculture
Director General of Water and Forests

_____

FORESTRY INSTITUTE
OF
RESEARCH AND EXPERIMENTS

Madrid April 9, 1956

Mr. Navarra:

According to your request of January 21, 1956 to our service, I am enclosing from our Forestry Institute a study and the scientific classification of a sample of wood fossil, observations of the section of wood, its nature, and conclusions.

Doctor J. Jimenez Herrara
Director

Study and Scientific Classification of a Wood Fossil Sample

The examination of a sample of wood given by Dr. Julian Jimenez Herrera, PhD in Chemistry, for Mr Fernand Navarra from Bordeaux, France, so that we may determine:

A. The forestry species to which it belongs
B. The approximate age
C. If this wood was worked with tools of stone, bronze, or iron.

And also, as a consequence, the study of the wood structure, and several physical characteristics, as follows:

REPORT

A. Scientific Classification of the Wood Sample

I. Structure of the wood—The examination of the ligneous structure shows a main mass composed of weak-lighted and thick-walled tissue fibers; in a slight magnification, these fibers seem closed, but the light is perfectly visible with a 100X magnification.

The pithy sections are of two kinds: uni-sectioned and short, and multi-sectioned and long-shaped.

The veins may be grouped in two categories: of a large diameter with the thylles very marked, visible to the naked eye and situated in the first layers of cells with varied growth. They are grouped in rows of from one to three.

The others have a slighter diameter and are grouped forming tongues or flames in a radial direction.

The parenchymal cells have a stronger light and thinner walls than the fiber cells; they are arranged in little uni-sectioned rows in the same direction as the annual rings.

Finally, the annual growth rings, very pronounced, are visible at first glance and show, at the edge of the autumn-growth zone, one or two rows of fibers with a flat mark in the radial direction.

II. Physical Characteristics—The piece of wood examined shows two areas of completely different consistencies; one, the outer area, seems plainly changed, and one can easily detach with a fingernail little fragments of tissue beginning to decompose.

The inner area shows a hard and compact wood, with a black color and is easily polished; the density of the wood is 1.100.

III. Preparation for the Microscope—The area of hard, sound wood was able to be cut into a microsection without tearing the tissues, as it appeared in the three cuts of the original board.

IV. Scientific Classification of the Wood Sample Examined— From the study of the wood structure which we have described, it is clear that the wood studied belongs to the species *Quercus pedunculata* Ehrh.

To corroborate everything discovered in these scientific analyses, we introduced a second board with the wood structure of a *Quercus pedunculata* from our laboratory's collection, showing its similarity to the sample of the first board.

B. AGE OF THE WOOD SAMPLE

Two traits may serve as a base for calculation, with all the margin for error proper in this case to ascertain the possible age of the wood examined: the density and the color.

The density of the sample seems to have a value of 1.100, and as the normal density of this wood is between 0.800 and 0.850, it is evident that this sample is in the lignitization phase of fossilization.

The color, which tells unquestionably the raised percentage of tannin normal in oak wood, confirms on its part its previous state.

Consequently, one can suppose the age of the wood sample given varies around five thousand years.

APPENDIX V

C. Tools with Which the Wood Was Worked

From the piece of wood examined, one cannot ascertain the category of the tools, of iron or of wood, with which the said sample was fashioned.

F. Nasera
Engineer, Head of the Forestry Section

The University of Bordeaux
Faculty of Sciences
Department of Anthropology & Prehistoric Studies

Anatomical Study of a Piece of Sub-Fossil Wood

Mr. Navarra, has given my laboratory a piece of sub-fossil wood gathered by him in the course of his explorations; our examination has resulted in the following findings:

I. Exterior Appearance:

The block seems to us as very lignitic and, on the other hand, corroded and cracked on the surface, the physical state resembling that of posts and dugout canoes, found in the palafittes on the Swiss lakes and preserved in the museums of that country, notably the one in Zurich.

According to the annual rings, this wood fragment was taken from a tree whose heartwood attained a diameter of at least 50 cm.

128

DOCUMENTATION ON THE WOOD TESTING

II. ZEISS' STEREO-MICROSCOPE EXAMINATION:

1. Transverse Cut—

Our impression of a very extensive lignation was confirmed. The thickness of the group of annual rings is varied, oscillating between 2 and 5 cm.

Primary pithy sections are multi-sectioned, with cells clearly elongated in a radial direction.

Secondary pithy sections are uni-sectioned, with cells less elongated in a radial direction.

The cells of both are rich in tannins.

2. Longitudinal Radial Cut—

A few weak veins give markings of oblique crevasses. In the lignitic fibers, the partition markings appear clearly. Different elements of ligneous parenchyma to the cells in the longitudinal direction give areolated markings on their lateral partitions.

The primary pithy sections are formed of long cells, generally terminated by oblique membrane which, for most of these cells, looks like a parallelogram or an elongated trapezoid.

The secondary pithy sections have relatively short rectangular cells, giving the group of pithy sections a wall-like appearance, which is characteristic. The walls of these cells are thicker and more clearly marked.

3. Longitudinal Tangential Cut—

Fat marked veins overgrown by the thyllose. It is the same for the veins of a weaker caliber belonging, for the most part, to autumn wood.

129

APPENDIX V

The thick veins of spring wood are of a strong caliber and grouped in a small number of rows, three at a maximum and arranged in irregular radial rows.

The autumn wood is very compact, with a lot of fibers and relatively few veins, accompanied by ligneous parenchyma.

The appearance of this autumn wood has become a little homogeneous by the high degree of lignition.

Primary pithy sections have, in most cases, a regulated and considerable width.

Secondary pithy sections are numerous, thin, and shorter than those preceding.

III. MICROSCOPIC EXAMINATION:

Transverse Cut—

Spring wood: marked veins, of a very great diameter, arranged in a small number of tangential rows, most of them over-grown by the thyllose. They are accompanied by a ligneous parenchyma with walls moderately thick and rich in tannoid cells.

Autumn wood: veins of a small caliber, immersed in a ligneous parenchyma of small cells (some of which are tannoids) and arranged in radial uni-sectioned rows. There is a great abundance of ligneous fibers in weak light and thick walls crossed with furrows. Most of these fibers are grouped in cellular blocks. Primary pithy sections form a considerable cellular block. Secondary pithy sections are very numerous, but uni-sectioned, spinkle-shaped in circumference but more reduced in width.

IV. RESULT OF THE SEPARATION BY MACERATION: BY SCHULTZE

The result of this preparation has confirmed, in the separated parts, the conclusions drawn in the cuts, and notably among the most significant:

—Presence of veins of a weak caliber shows markings of oblique crevasses.

—Presence of areolated markings on the lateral walls of certain parts of the ligneous parenchyma in the long cells.

V. CLASSIFICATION OF THE WOOD

By all the characteristics observed and noted above, this wood belongs without any doubt to a *Quercus* of a group of oaks with deciduous leaves.

Certain particular characteristics seem to dismiss the species most frequently studied in France.

The absence of a regular decrease of thick veins of spring wood toward the formation of autumn wood dismisses the peduncular oak: *Quercus pedunculata* Ehrh., and moreover the Austrian oak: *Quercus sessilis* Ehrh.

On the contrary, it seems that one can associate it with the fibrous oak, *Quercus cerris* L., considering the radial uni-sectioned rows following which the autumn wood veins are arranged.

This beautiful tree of the peri-Mediterranean region has moreover a heavy and compact wood, of an average density of 0.925 which, in times of wooden ships, was used in the Orient for naval construction.

It is nevertheless permissible to hesitate between this oak and the *Quercus castaneifolia* Mey., from the south and east Mediterranean regions, whose wood shows an extremely close anatomical structure, with an average density of 0.938.

VI. ECOLOGICAL CHARACTERISTICS

The analysis of the annual rings suggests a tree with an active growth, having grown in a forest of little density, in a climate with seasons well separated, with spring very humid, followed by a much dryer summer and autumn.

VII. DEGREE OF LIGNITIZATION

The advanced stage of lignitization deserves to be noted; one can conclude that this wood was subject to conditions very favorable to fossilization, during a period dating to a remote antiquity.

April 15, 1956

G. Malvesin-Fabre
Professor, Faculty of the Sciences
Director of Prehistoric Institute of
the University of Bordeaux

Center for Forestry Research and Analysis
Paris, France

Classification of a Wood Sample

Leafy wood from a porous area, formed with thick veins obstructed by thylles.

Veins of the wood end are arranged in radiating flames.

Simultaneous presence of uni-sections and multi-sections.

It is clearly the heart of the wood of a deciduous oak. This wood is identical to that of a linnean oak *Quercus robur* L. It could belong to *Quercus pedunculata* Ehrh.

The Head of the Biology Division
C I Jacquiot

(undated—1956?), ed.

Newberg, Oregon
January 27, 1959

M. Fernand Navarra
84, Boulevard George V
Bordeaux, France

Dear Sir:

Thank you for your letter of November 14, 1958; I am grateful for the information you reported in it. I will be happy to read your book when it is published in English. Right now, I am happy to have an excellent résumé of it, which one of my friends translated into English. After having read this résumé, several times, I wanted to discuss a few points relative to the Ark and its site on Mount Ararat, etc.

As you have suggested in the book, it seems improbable that the flood waters left the Ark at its present height. You've probably heard of the discoveries of geologists who have proven that region of Mt Ararat is more elevated now than before. The present height of this mountain certainly comes from the increasing thrust of the earth's crust in this region. In keeping with this fact, Arctic seals have been discovered in the Baikal Lake and in the Caspian Sea, which would indicate that these waters joined with the Arctic Ocean at one time.

You probably know that they have frequently found well-preserved bodies of Mastadons and other animals in the Siberian ice and in North America. Many of these animals were discovered with grass undigested in their stomach. This proves two things:

1. That at one time there was abundant vegetation in these arid lands, now glaciers, and,

2. That these herbivores were stricken quickly and killed by an enormous snowfall at the beginning of the glacial period.

One can only explain these two aforesaid conclusions assuming that at one time the earth was surrounded by a vast canopy of water causing a new greenness on the earth. The first chapter of Genesis confirms this theory which mentions "the waters above the firmament." Conforming to this theory, the waters amassed above the polar regions where the centrifugal force was smaller up to the time when the canopy burst, permitting these furious waters to fall. With the rupture of this canopy an extreme cold in the polar regions provoked an immediate change. The water fell as rain in the tropical regions, but in the polar region, where the water was more concentrated, it fell in enormous quantities of snow.

As another corroboration in Genesis, one may note chapter 2, verses 5 and 6, which say that there was no rain in the Antediluvian period but, "There went up a mist from the earth, and watered the whole face of the ground." The first rainbow was observed by Noah after having left the Ark. All these reasons serve to prove the theory of the canopy which was first proposed by Isaac N. Vail in 1894. That's why this is known as the 'Vailian' theory.

Apparently the descent of this enormous weight of water on the surface of the planet caused a great change on the earth's crust. The seas were deepened and the mountains raised. There isn't any other way of explaining the receding flood waters quoted in Genesis. The great masses of ice which were formed in the northern and southern zones are also an important factor. There is about a century that the central part of the North American continent went through an enormous earthquake. This is recognized by geologists as the reversal of the earth's crust. This phenomenon is sometimes considered as substantial evidence of the beginning of the glacial period.

Apparently the book of Genesis consists chiefly of a compilation of genealogical records with editorial comments by Moses as P. J. Wiseman has shown in his book *New Discoveries from Genesis to Babylon*. These frank genealogical records of contemporary events are of the same point of view as those who have written it. An exception is the account of the creation in the first and second chapter, which one can explain only as being divine revelations to Adam.

I am personally convinced that the Bible is in effect what it claims, to the letter: Divine revelation to man. Without a doubt your opinion is similar to inspire you to persevering research—a conviction that the Ark itself is a prophecy and its remains are a monument to the foresight and wisdom of God.

As suggested formerly, the icy grounds of the southern regions of the North American continent contain formal evidence of a great cataclysm which caused the glacial period. Wouldn't it be extremely interesting if we could prove that the organic remains of the Pleistocenes were from the same time period as your fragments of Noah's Ark?

Pursuing this idea, I've started negotiations with the authorities in Alaska to obtain some of this material. If my efforts are successful, would you be interested if we could examine this material in the same laboratory in which they examined your specimen of the Ark? I would be happy to pay the necessary expenses without wishing to be associated with you since I am not associated with your research in any way. My goal isn't personal fame, but rather progress, and the exculpation of the truth.

Summing up, let me say that I am very happy to read that the exact age of the wood which has been dated by the 'radiocarbon' process was 4484 years old. This age agrees with the strict chronology of the Bible, and can be expressed in the following way:

Date of the flood (BC)	2472
Date in which the Ark was found	1955
Number of years from the flood to 1955	4427
Number of years wood was cut before the flood	57
Total age of the wood when it was examined	4484

Awaiting your reply, I am most respectfully yours.

CARLTON YEREX

Route 3, Box M75
Sherwood, OR 97140
January 12, 1971

Mr Fernand Navarra
84, Boulevard George V
Bordeaux, France

Dear Sir,

I received your form letter May 11, 1959. I've thought of you often in these intervening years, in your expedition to Mount Ararat to find the Ark, and the attention you drew in your last expedition. I was often surprised; what is your next project?

Last year I heard your name in relation to your expedition, with other explorers. The letter says that this expedition is cancelled for military reasons.

Do you think the Turkish restrictions are loosened? It may be possible to undertake this expedition.

I send my best regards, and hope for your success.

Your sincere Friend,
CARLETON YEREX